Summary of Contents

C000295715

JUMP START PHP ENVIRONMENT

BY BRUNO ŠKVORC

Jump Start PHP Environment

by Bruno Škvorc

Copyright © 2015 SitePoint Pty. Ltd.

Product Manager: Simon Mackie

English Editor: Kelly Steele

Cover Designer: Alex Walker

Notice of Rights

Notice of Liability

Trademark Notice

Published by SitePoint Pty. Ltd.

48 Cambridge Street Collingwood
VIC Australia 3066
Web: www.sitepoint.com
Email: business@sitepoint.com

ISBN 978-0-9941826-4-7 (print)

ISBN 978-0-9943469-5-7 (ebook)
Printed and bound in the United States of America

About Bruno Škvorc

Bruno, a web developer from Croatia, is SitePoint's senior PHP editor by day, and a developer evangelist for Diffbot.com by night. A big fan of working on treadmill desks, he spends the most of his days walking through various projects and problems, and then exposing them on SitePoint.com. In his free time (i.e. when his beagle is asleep) he swims, #stronglifts, plays (board) games and paints miniatures.

About SitePoint

SitePoint specializes in publishing fun, practical, and easy-to-understand content for web professionals. Visit http://www.sitepoint.com/ to access our blogs, books, newsletters, articles, and community forums. You'll find a stack of information on JavaScript, PHP, Ruby, mobile development, design, and more.

To my beautiful Mateja, and adorable Rita, without whom this book would have been written much sooner

Table of Contents

Chapter 3 **The Application Environment** 29

Chapter 4 **Virtual Machines** 43

Preface

The WWW

In this section, I will answer the three Ws. No, not *that* www—the three Ws of this book:

- Why was this book written?
- What's it about?
- Who is it for?

The What and Why

Before I explain who the book is for, I'd like to start by explaining what this book is about and what prompted its writing.

The Why

As the editor for SitePoint's PHP channel[1], I communicate daily with many PHP developers. Almost every developer comes from a different background—educational, racial, geographical—so the channel is truly a melting pot of cultures and approaches. Some are formally trained computer scientists, others are self-taught freelancers. Some are well-versed in enterprise etiquette, rigor, and culture; others just can't wait to just churn out code and see it work. In all of my time working for SitePoint, I've never once met two developers who have the same approach to writing and coding.

Trying to create a channel that works cohesively with such an array or writers was actually quite challenging. The writing part was easy to standardize—I enforced the Markdown format (no need to concern yourself with this if you don't know what it is) rather than HTML or Word files, passed on some links to valuable tools such as spell-checkers and text smell detectors (tools that capitalize your title, check for repeated phrases, isolate misused phrases, and so on). But when you're responsible for editing and checking hundreds of posts, it's not the writing that's the biggest problem—it's the code. Writers would send their code in zip archives alongside their articles, as if thrown into a cardboard box, duct-taped, and shipped.

---

[1] http://www.sitepoint.com/php/

The code was everything from simply messy to incompatible with my version of PHP, and thus it was insanely difficult to verify—after all, letting a malfunctioning demo go live alongside a tutorial would be unforgivable! Imagine receiving code samples from 100 different people, each configured for a separate combination of PHP + server + PHP extensions and other factors. There's simply no way to manually configure your computer fast enough to be able to go through them all reliably in a given time frame. Code needs standardization, and in big teams, such as ours in SitePoint's PHP channel, this is of utmost importance.

To remove this barrier, I used all the approaches I talk about in this book. To make them work for you and to have code that is automatically compatible with all other developers and their computers instantly would be minutes of work; however, this book was written to help you understand *what* is going on in these configurations, and *how* exactly this compatibility was achieved. Why would you want to know this, you might wonder?

Two reasons:

1. You'll gain a solid foundation extremely early in your career, absorbing good practices before you've had a chance to be exposed to bad ones. I cannot stress enough how important this is; the amount of energy it takes to unlearn something is colossal, especially if you're told *you're wrong*, because we have a natural predisposition to take a defensive stance—even if, deep down, we might know the other party is right.

2. If you're serious about building a PHP career, chances are you'll end up leading or joining a team of developers one day. Maybe it will be a freelance team building small websites for individual clients; perhaps you'll lead fifty people in an enterprise effort to modernize a corporation's intranet application—who knows, but you'll have to work with other developers eventually. Trust me when I tell you that you won't be a one-man army forever (or at all!). When working with others, it's vitally important you all have the exact same software setup in order to prevent excuses such as "What do you mean broken? It works on my machine!" With the instructions as laid out in this book, you'll understand completely what's necessary to set this up team-wide. Your team will thank you in the long run, even if you'll initially slow down progress by making everyone adapt to these practices.

With that out of the way, what *will* we be learning in this tome?

The What

This book will, in great detail, explain what you need to do to *prepare to start learning PHP*. This might sound confusing (preparing for a start?), so let me explain.

Most people, when they become interested in web development, randomly google for keywords and click the first results they find; "how to make a website," "build php mysql site tutorial," and "learn to code," the search queries will say. Inevitably, almost all newbies end up downloading XAMPP or WAMP (installer tools that get PHP and associated packages set up on your machine), setting up a basic PHP installation on their computers, and writing the legendary Hello World "app." Without fail, this is where over 70% of the newbies are lost. XAMPP, WAMP, EasyPHP, and similar bundles that get you up and running fast are—while practical at first—deterrents in the long run. We'll talk about this in more depth in later chapters, but suffice to say that while these bundles are easy to start, but hard to continue with, this book takes the exact opposite approach: more complex to start, but easy to keep going.

I'll show you how to configure your development environment in such a way that you'll be able to develop without worrying about impacting anything on your computer or its operating system, and can share your code with others without concern about whether it will be compatible with their setup. What's more, you'll be able to build and test applications for various versions of PHP without needing to reinstall anything: your different versions of PHP will never conflict, and you can even test your applications on different web servers as well.

Your code will be cross-platform compatible, meaning you'll be able to run it and keep developing it anywhere you go, no matter which computer you land on or which operating system powers it. I'll teach you about the powers of a good IDE (integrated development environment), explain the powerful concepts of application environments, show you the mysteries of virtual machines, and prepare you for the professional PHP world.

If any of these terms sound intimidating or complex to you right now, don't despair. We'll cover *all* of them later on. You *will* understand everything, that's a promise.

The Who

So, who is this book for?

Developers of beginner to intermediate level will benefit from this book. Even for those familiar with some of the concepts, this book will hold some value. Remember, everyone you ever meet will know something you don't. You can always learn more, even if most of it sounds familiar.

If you are interested in improving your current development workflow and often find yourself confused by missing PHP extensions or features while developing applications, and frequently running into errors about software you need but are yet to install—this book is for you. If your computer is so full of software used to make other people's code run well on your machine, this book is definitely for you. By reading it, you'll be able to restore your computer to an almost factory level of performance while keeping all apps you come across compatible with it.

If you're just starting out with PHP, this book should be the very first resource you read. It will explain not only isolated development environments and conflict prevention, but also the inner workings of web requests and what happens when you actually type an address into a browser's address bar. You'll learn why a server is important, what PHP's role is, and how it all fits into the grand scheme of development environments and setups that can help you achieve a smooth development experience.

Note that this is not a programming book, *per se*. There will be very little PHP coding in this book, at least until the very end of it. This book is a guide to setting up your computer so that it obeys you, rather than the other way around. You want programming to be a pleasant, relaxing, and predictable experience you can train yourself in, day by day, rather than a source of endless frustration. That is what this book is for—laying the foundation for a pleasant programming career.

Conventions Used

You'll notice that we've used certain typographic and layout styles throughout this book to signify different types of information. Look out for the following items.

Code Samples

Code in this book is displayed using a fixed-width font, like so:

```
<h1>A Perfect Summer's Day</h1>
<p>It was a lovely day for a walk in the park. The birds
were singing and the kids were all back at school.</p>
```

If the code is to be found in the book's code archive, the name of the file will appear at the top of the program listing, like this:

```
                                                         example.css
.footer {
  background-color: #CCC;
  border-top: 1px solid #333;
}
```

If only part of the file is displayed, this is indicated by the word *excerpt*:

```
                                                 example.css (excerpt)
  border-top: 1px solid #333;
```

If additional code is to be inserted into an existing example, the new code will be displayed in bold:

```
function animate() {
  new_variable = "Hello";
}
```

Where existing code is required for context, rather than repeat all of it, ⋮ will be displayed:

```
function animate() {
  ⋮
  return new_variable;
}
```

Some lines of code should be entered on one line, but we've had to wrap them because of page constraints. An ➡ indicates a line break that exists for formatting purposes only, and should be ignored:

```
URL.open("http://www.sitepoint.com/responsive-web-design-real-user-
➡testing/?responsive1");
```

Tips, Notes, and Warnings

Hey, You!

Tips provide helpful little pointers.

Ahem, Excuse Me ...

Notes are useful asides that are related—but not critical—to the topic at hand. Think of them as extra tidbits of information.

Make Sure You Always ...

... pay attention to these important points.

Watch Out!

Warnings highlight any gotchas that are likely to trip you up along the way.

Supplementary Materials

https://www.sitepoint.com/premium/books/phpenv1
The book's website, containing links, updates, resources, and more.

https://github.com/spbooks/phpenv1-example/
The downloadable code archive for this book.

http://community.sitepoint.com/
SitePoint's forums, for help on any tricky web problems.

books@sitepoint.com

> Our email address, should you need to contact us for support, to report a problem, or for any other reason.

Want to take your learning further?

Thanks for choosing to buy a SitePoint book. Would you like to continue learning? You can now gain unlimited access to ALL SitePoint books and courses plus high-quality books from our selected partners at SitePoint Premium.[2] Enroll now and start learning today!

---

[2] https://www.sitepoint.com/premium/home

The Anatomy of Web Requests

Before we get into the nitty-gritty of setting up a good PHP environment, you need an understanding of how web requests actually work. This chapter will explain what happens when you punch a web address into your browser and receive a result. We'll avoid being *too* technical—there's no need to explain the nuts and bolts, as it would likely only confuse you. Instead, it will be a newbie-friendly explanation on how all the various aspects of web development and web consumption come together and create the Web you know and love. The main purpose of this chapter is to teach you where your programming language of choice (in this case, PHP) comes into play, and which parts of the mysterious *web request* it affects.

If you know the essentials of the Web and are familiar with the terms mentioned in the previous paragraph, feel free to jump to the next chapter.

The Client and the Server

You must have heard of the terms "client-side programming" and "server-side programming," at least in job ads. In this part, we'll briefly explain them before moving onto the details.

What is a client?

A **client** is your web browser.

In the context of the Web, while you *are* technically the client in the conventional sense of the word (you are doing the requesting and being served by software), the browser is considered to be the **client software** used to ask the server for something.

Once it receives this "something" (most often being a bunch of text), it decides how it should present it to you, the ultimate client.

What is a server?

Similar to the client, a **server** also has two meanings:

1. a *program* that answers questions posed by the client
2. a computer (a physical machine) onto which the *server program* is installed

In this book, and in the context of web development, we generally mean the former. In fact, throughout this book, we'll learn how we can easily install a server program on our own computer, essentially "faking the Internet" and letting the computer think the website we're developing is online and accessible by everyone.

Let's look at the first point a bit more: how does a program answer questions?

In a nutshell, a server waits for a question such as "give me the text of the blog post from February 14th" and responds with either "OK, here: [some HTML, containing the text oft the post in question]" or "Sorry, I can't find that, there's nothing under February 14th." Admittedly, I'm paraphrasing, but that's more or less what happens. I've illustrated it in Figure 1.1.

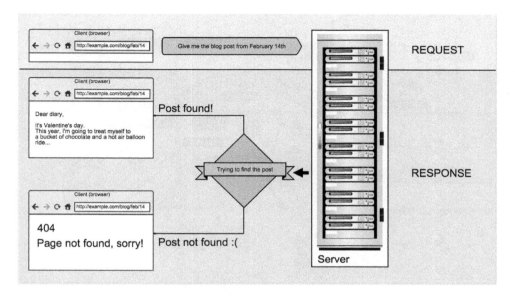

Figure 1.1. A simplified request to the server and its response

Web development is, in fact, a relatively simple matter of making the client ask the right questions, and teaching the server to give the right responses. Ready to go a little bit deeper into the rabbit hole? Here goes ...

Web Request Basics

While **web request** has a very specific meaning, it is often used as a blanket term for the communication between the client and the server. This entire communication process is neatly explained in Figure 1.2, a cute comic by VladStudio.[1]

---

[1] http://www.vladstudio.com/wallpaper/?how_internet_works

Figure 1.2. *How Internet Works* by VladStudio

How It All Works

Let's break the comic in Figure 1.2 down.

You are the user—you are the king. You issue the commands and the browser obeys, happily. As the user, this is where your awareness of the process ends, and the next time you're consciously addressed is in the second-to-last frame of the comic. The entire process in between is invisible to you, except when you're a developer; then you're a magic wizard king who can see everything that's happening, but more on that in later chapters.

The browser goes through a firewall, which is usually taken for granted. You probably have some manner of firewall on your computer right now, or in your router/modem. The browser knows how to pass through it because you've told the guard the browser is okay and should be let through.

Then comes a part we've yet to mention: the **DNS (domain name system)** servers—a part so mystical and unapproachable to most, the vast majority of internet users (and developers, even!) take it for granted, accept that it exists, and try not to worry about it too much. The general consensus seems to be that, like questions about the meaning of life, queries about the origin of time and space, and the otherworldly deliciousness of peanut butter and banana combo, some things—such as the origin and purpose of DNS servers—are better left unquestioned. If you'd still like to know what they are, they'll be explained in the section called "For Those Who Want More" at the end of this chapter in greater detail.

In a nutshell, this is how they work. Every **domain** on the Internet (like "example.com") is bound to a specific IP address (represented by the numbers on the signpost in the third frame of the comic). An **IP address** is a set of numbers identifying a given server; IP addresses tell the browser how to navigate the Internet to find the computer (server) it's looking for.

Remember longitude and latitude from geography classes? They specifically define a geographical point on planet Earth, and are cross-country compatible, meaning anyone from anywhere will know how to a find a location if you give them the latitude and longitude values; however, we also have a human-friendly description for the most popular coordinates. For example, the name of the town I went to university in is Rijeka. Not many people will know where to find it on a map, but if I give them the coordinates (45.3167° N, 14.4167° E),[2] they can easily locate it. A DNS server is a translator, a guide. This server knows which IP addresses match which domain name, and tells the browser where to go next.

Once redirected to a specific IP address, the browser knocks on the door of the hosting server. This particular server was mentioned in the previous section, and we refer to it only as "the server." The browser brings with it the information that the user requested and asks the server for an answer to the question "google.com?". The server answers: "Yes, under google.com, the file says ..." and gives the answer. The browser returns to the user (the king) and conveys the information. This part is what's important for us developers—telling the server what answer to give for a specific question. Remember this part.

Front-end and Back-end

It's time to define two more terms you must have heard at least once. **Front-end development** (also called client-side development) focuses on work with the client

---

[2] http://bit.ly/rijekageo

software, while **back-end development** (also called server-side development) deals with the server software.

When a server returns text to your browser (in Figure 1.2, this is the text that's repeated to the king in the second-to-last frame) and your browser presents it to you, how that text *looks* and in what ways you can *interact with it* is front-end (or client-side) programming. When you open a website and a link is bold and a different color to the rest of the text, that change in appearance was achieved with client-side programming (HTML plus CSS). When you can drag an element around on the screen or initiate animations or sounds, it's also achieved with client-side programming (specifically HTML and CSS accompanied by JavaScript).

Server-side programming, or back-end development, is the action of configuring the server computer and program (see the section called "What is a server?" for an explanation on this duality) to give back the appropriate data to the browser when asked. This typically means programming in a server-side language such as PHP. PHP will make some calculations or grab some data from a database, turn it into text that can be given to the browser, and the browser will take it and display it to the user.

Even though all content returned to the browser for delivery to the user is actually stored on the server, we call CSS and JavaScript "client-side" because their calculations happen *in the browser*. For example, if I told JavaScript to animate a square turning into a circle, the math behind the calculation will be happening in the browser. The server will only provide the formula and tell the browser: "When you take this back to your king, say it like this ..." On the other hand, server-side programming implies that all logic, calculations, formulas, and so on happen *on the server*, merely returning the end result. For example, if I have a website that counts the number of images uploaded by a user (such as Facebook counting the number of images in your album), this calculation will be done on the server, and only the final number will be given to the browser when it asks for this information.

To recap: front end is when you write code that is executed in the browser (HTML, CSS, JavaScript), while back end is when you write code that is executed on the server before passing the final result onto the browser. PHP, server-side JavaScript, server-side Dart, Ruby, Python, and other programming languages fit the bill.

Time to go even deeper into the rabbit hole.

Server-side Languages

This book focuses on preparing a development environment for server-side programming. We won't be dealing with HTML, CSS, or JavaScript; there are plenty of books on those out there, and setting up a client-side development flow is complex enough on its own. Instead, we'll be dealing exclusively with server-side preparations, as it's very easy to start off the wrong way. Just as a speck on a balloon will grow into a large stain as it fills with air, so too can a misstep in the beginning of a programming career grow into a long-term harmful habit.

As you may already know, examples of server-side languages include PHP, Ruby, and Python. They sit as programs on the server computer, as well as the server program. These languages take certain commands from the server program, and output the result of these commands back to it. It is this output that is given to the browser when a user asks for an answer to a certain question. In a nutshell, by telling the server "When a request comes in for the example.com website, run this file through PHP":

```php
<?php

echo "Hello World";
```

... we have given it a way to produce an answer for the client. The PHP file is then run, and the content "Hello World" is generated and sent back to the server program, which is then given to the browser. The browser takes it back to the user and simply repeats "Hello World." The browser stops short of relaying the rest of the contents of the file; the php tag `<?php` and the keyword `echo` are skipped in the output. This is because the tag `<?php` tells the server to "Run this file through PHP" and then, when running the file through PHP, `echo` tells it "Output the following phrase on-screen."

If you're having trouble grasping this, see Figure 1.3, which expands on Figure 1.1.

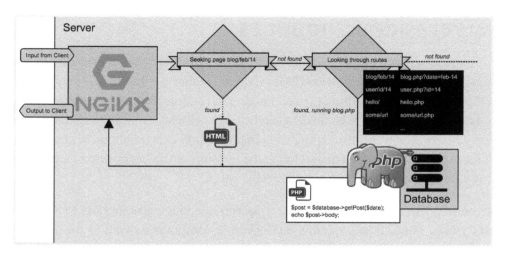

Figure 1.3. Server asks PHP for the answer if it's unable to find one

In Figure 1.3:

- the digram represents the insides of the physical computer in Figure 1.1
- Nginx is a web server program installed on this machine
- Nginx receives input from the client in the form of a question (blog for February 14th)
- Nginx checks if there's a page for `blog/feb/14`
- as there is none, Nginx checks the routes towards PHP files
- Nginx finds that it needs to run the `blog.php` script through PHP
- the `blog.php` script connects to the database and sends back the text for the given date
- the PHP engine sends this result to the server
- Nginx sends it back to the client

To recap: PHP is an answer generator for the server so it knows what answers to give to the browser's questions. This way, the server doesn't need to know the answers, it just knows that PHP does and asks it, then forwards the response to the browser. Imagine a "Hello YourName" page; it's impossible to generate pages for every existing name, but we can have PHP ask for a name on one page, and then generate the answer to give to the server on another page.

What's important to grasp here is the communication flow between client and server, and server and server-side language. This entire communication fits into the fifth and sixth frames in the comic in Figure 1.2. In fact, the part where the server program talks to the PHP program would happen entirely in the sixth frame.

Generating Answers with Server-side Languages

The last and deepest level of our rabbit hole is the actual conversation between the server program and a server-side language—in our case (and all future cases), PHP. We covered this to an extent in the previous section, but let's look at another example now with a situation of when an answer cannot be found.

Let's say that the server is asked the following by the client: "Can you get me whatever you have filed under `example.com/user/id/54`?" This is what happens next:

1. The server checks whether there's something already prepared under the route: `/user/id/54`. If there are no files to be found there, it's configured to ask PHP.
2. The server asks PHP: "Hey, can you find anything under `/user/id/54`?"
3. PHP activates and looks through its routes. Lo and behold, the route `/user/id/54` says "activate file `user.php` with the parameter `id` of value `54`."
4. PHP executes the file (the actual logic of the file is beside the point and outside the scope of this chapter) and receives a result. Maybe the result is the email address of the 54th user in the database. This email address is then given back to the server: "Sure, I found something under that route. The answer is: johndoe@example.com".
5. The server responds with "Thanks!" and passes this message on to the client, who then presents it to the end user—you.

However, what if there's nothing filed under that route? For example, there is a typo when the client requests `example.com/urer/id/54` (rather than "user"). Here's what happens:

1. The server checks whether there's anything already prepared under the route: `/urer/id/54`. If no files are found, it's configured to ask PHP.
2. The server asks PHP: "Can you find anything under `/urer/id/54`?"
3. PHP activates and looks through its routes, but fails to unearth anything. It returns a "404 Page not found" error to the server (as in Figure 1.1, bottom-left result). As you're most probably aware, 404 is a code that's common in web technologies and means that what you're looking for is unable to be found where you think it

might be. Many such status codes exist, but there's no need to know them all in this phase of your career.

4. The server receives the 404 message and thinks "Hmm, PHP lucked out. Well, it has nothing, I have nothing, better return a page to the client that says we were unsuccessful." The browser is then given a 404 page, which is usually just a textual warning such as "Whoops, you tried a wrong link!" but can also be as intricate as you want it to be.[3]

I trust that this chapter was clear with the concepts it presented and helped you get your bearings in terms of where you are (or will be) in the grand scheme of PHP programming. In the section that follows, you'll find some more technical information on web requests and DNS servers.

For Those Who Want More

DNS Servers

As mentioned before, every domain (such as example.com) on the Internet is bound to a specific IP address (such as 93.184.216.34). An IP address is a set of numbers identifying a given server. In other words, IP addresses tell the browser how to navigate the Internet to find the computer (server) it's looking for. A DNS server (also known as just name server) knows which IP addresses match which domain name, and tells the browser where to go next.

When trying to find out which IP address matches a domain name, the browser first checks its own **cache**—a saved list of previously visited domains. Every browser maintains this list and periodically refreshes it. If it finds the domain-IP combination in its own cache, the site loads faster because there's no need to ask the DNS server for it. If the domain isn't cached, the browser asks a program called the **resolver** (which is built into your operating system) to check the hosts file on the computer it's installed on. The hosts file is where the user can actually define which website maps to which IP address. (We'll be learning to use this file in later chapters.) If the necessary information isn't there, the DNS cache on the router (routers usually have one, too) is checked, and if it's not found there either, the ISP company's DNS server is asked.

---

[3] http://www.creativebloq.com/web-design/best-404-pages-812505

Up until that last step, everything was happening on your own computer, or, as we say, *locally*. Now that it's time to visit the ISP, it's no longer a local matter—it's remote. If the ISP's DNS server is without a record for the domain, it finds out and tells the browser, then caches the results for future queries. How does it find out? It dissects the domain name from right to left.

www.example.com is split up into fragments. The .com part, called the **TLD** or **top-level domain**, is first. There are many DNS servers around the world, often configured in such a way that multiple computers act as one. This is so that if one dies, others ensure the service is uninterrupted. The highest level of these servers are **root servers**, which know where to further look for details about a domain on any given TLD. The root server with the appropriate records for .com will know that it's a dot com, so will send you a query further in XYZ—XYZ being another name server that will know the `example` part. Further still, the www part (also known as the **subdomain**) will come into play, and be registered on a specific name server, too, in this confusing chain of names and servers. Once all the fragments (also known as labels: .com, example, and www) are resolved into an IP address, the result is sent back.

If you'd like to know more about root name servers and want to find out how the entire Internet's smooth functioning depends on thirteen main computers (well, clusters of computers), take a look the root name server page on Wikipedia,[4] or check out some amazingly comprehensive answers on Super User.[5]

What Happens When You Type ...

A common programmer job interview question is "What happens when you type google.com into your browser's address box and press enter?" While, in part, we explained this earlier (albeit in a simplified manner), check out Alex Gaynor's excellent description if you'd like to know the exact details,[6] from hardware to end software. It's an extremely comprehensive but very well-written post. Note that, realistically, this level of detailed knowledge is unnecessary to be a good developer.

---

[4] https://en.wikipedia.org/wiki/Root_name_server

[5] http://superuser.com/questions/527116/how-does-my-browser-locate-the-nearest-dns-root-servers

[6] https://github.com/alex/what-happens-when

2

The Programming Environment

There are two types of environment in the context of programming: the application environment, and the programming environment. We'll be covering the application environment in a later chapter. This part of the book will talk about the **programming environment**, explaining IDEs (integrated development environments) and suggesting which ones to try, explaining coding standards and exploring some command line basics. In this chapter, it all becomes slightly more technical.

The programming environment includes—but is not limited to—the people you interact with, your operating system, your code editor or IDE (more on this later), your coding standards, and generally everything that helps or hinders your work *during development*. In other words, the programming environment is the *programmer's* environment.

Skip this chapter if you:

▨ have a good IDE picked out and don't intend to switch

▨ know where to find help for any programming problems

▨ are following coding standards already, whether you're in a team or flying solo are familiar with the command line

Read this chapter if you:

are using a simple text editor to code or don't know any IDEs

think coding standards are unnecessary

have no idea where to obtain genuinely useful advice for problems you might encounter

are unfamiliar with the command line and/or think it's unnecessary because alternatives exist

A Good IDE Is Worth Its File Size in Gold

The old adage of "being worth its own weight in gold" stands true for **IDEs**, or **integrated development environments**. IDEs are advanced programs for writing code, and at the end of this section we'll present a few decent options for you to try.

You may be familiar with text editors such as TextMate or Notepad. There are code-oriented alternatives such as Sublime Text[1] and Notepad++[2] that make coding much, much easier by offering commonly known language constructs and helping you autocomplete some statements so that memorizing entire programming language commands is a thing of the past. Most even offer **syntax highlighting**, which makes code more readable by applying different colors to certain keywords and phrases that are programming-language-specific. See Figure 2.1 for code without syntax highlighting, and Figure 2.2 for an example with syntax highlighting.

---

[1] http://www.sublimetext.com/

[2] https://notepad-plus-plus.org/

```php
<?php

class test
{
    protected $name;

    /**
     * Show the application welcome screen to the user.
     *
     * @return Response
     */
    public function index()
    {
        $provider = new Google([
            'clientId'     => '322309742012-7uq72vjsgh0prldthb7pc4elpeu6bh64.apps.googleusercontent.com',
            'clientSecret' => 'Xtc0S4UoWYUKTZy6Er2GnHxf',
            'redirectUri'  => 'http://todohelpist-local.com:8000/',
            'scopes'       => ['email'],
        ]);

        $provider->doStuff();
    }
}
```

Figure 2.1. Text editor without syntax highlighting

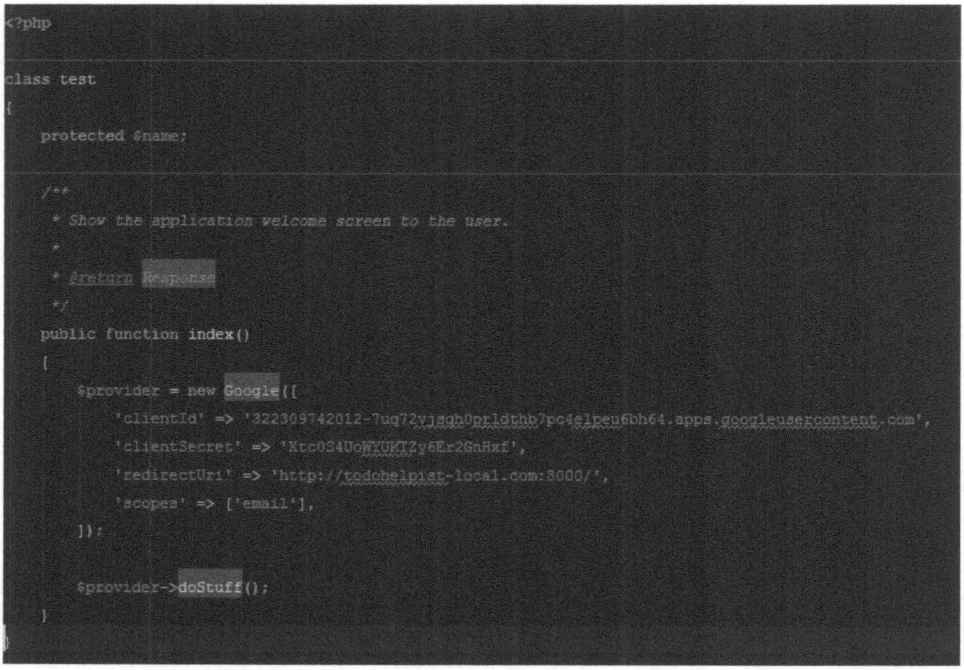

```php
<?php

class test
{
    protected $name;

    /**
     * Show the application welcome screen to the user.
     *
     * @return Response
     */
    public function index()
    {
        $provider = new Google([
            'clientId' => '322309742012-7uq72yjsqh0prldthb7pc4elpeu6bh64.apps.googleusercontent.com',
            'clientSecret' => 'Xtc034UoWYUKTZy6Er2GnHxf',
            'redirectUri' => 'http://todohelpist-local.com:8000/',
            'scopes' => ['email'],
        ]);

        $provider->doStuff();
    }
}
```

Figure 2.2. Text editor with syntax highlighting

Yet without exception, all text editors pale in comparison to good IDEs. An IDE is a powerful program—it's like a text editor on steroids containing in-depth references to your given language of choice, often helping you by providing suggestions and coloring the text to make it more readable, as well as by:

- helping you automatically apply coding standards to your code (we'll discuss coding standards later in this chapter)

- allowing you to move code up and down or left and right, and easily duplicate it without having to cut and paste

- supplying coding templates so you that can avoid rewriting the same commands over and over again

- providing intricate search facilities that treat various commands and functions as entities and not just text, meaning you can do things like tell the IDE "Show me where this function first appears"

- integrating bug checkers, standards checkers, and testing suites, all of which ensure that your application is running properly without you having to constantly recheck it

- integrating version control systems so that you can maintain different versions of your code from the IDE, ensuring that you always have infinite "undo" capabilities when programming (more on version control in Chapter 5)

- enabling you to connect to databases and remote servers right from the IDE, letting you easily debug your database or test the code on your remote server (for example, a company's server at headquarters while you're at home) to ensure it will work fine come Monday morning

And much, much more.

So, which IDEs are a good option for PHP development?

In my own order of preference:

PhpStorm

PhpStorm[3] is a commercial IDE, meaning it's neither open source nor free, but it's well worth the price. It offers everything that's been mentioned above and more, and works on all operating systems flawlessly, whether you're on Linux, Windows, or Mac OS X. It has been written about on SitePoint extensively[4] if you'd like to see some reviews, handy shortcuts, hacks to become even more efficient, other people's approaches, and so on. JetBrains—the company who makes it—also tends to give out free licenses now and then, and you can qualify for one by maintaining an open-source project. Alternatively, keep an eye out for surveys and reviews on SitePoint's PHP channel[5] as we sometimes give out licenses, too.

Commercial support means quick responses from the support team, rapid development (updates come out regularly with many new features), and a guarantee of continued maintenance. Note that PhpStorm allows for a 30-day free trial, and if you're still yet to be convinced after a month, they'll often extend your trial license.

---

[3] https://www.jetbrains.com/phpstorm/

[4] http://www.sitepoint.com/tag/phpstorm/

[5] http://sitepoint.com/php

Pros: very fast, feature-rich, stable (never crashes), cross-platform support

Cons: costs money, can be resource-intensive, and is unfriendly to older computers. See requirements at
https://www.jetbrains.com/phpstorm/help/system-requirements-and-installation.html.

NetBeans

NetBeans[6], an open-source IDE, sports almost all the features of PhpStorm and is its nemesis. I had used NetBeans for two years before transitioning to PhpStorm, and recommend it to everyone who needs a good IDE but isn't prepared to pay for a commercial one.

NetBeans is slightly slower than PhpStorm and more resource-intensive. It is cross-platform, relatively stable, and very reliable. The group behind it was acquired by Oracle, and while some see this as a bad omen, I feel it only cements the reliability of the current version.

Pros: free, feature-rich, reliable, cross-platform, open source

Cons: Oracle-owned, lacks commercial support, slower to adopt new features

Zend Studio

Zend Studio[7] is made by the company "in charge" of PHP (though, it's been acquired by Rogue Wave software, whose name may appear in certain places where Zend used to be). Zend is the company who first brought PHP into existence, and who provide official certification for the language.

Zend Studio is a commercial IDE that's a bit pricier than PhpStorm, but it offers a free trial so you can give it a spin before committing to it. It has many of the same features of PhpStorm and NetBeans, with some exceptions, as well as some of its own. Tools for easier mobile app development (available in Netbeans and PhpStorm via plugins) are built into Zend Studio, and its own Apigility platform (a service for creating APIs based on their Zend Framework) has a native Zend Studio driver, too. Don't worry if you're unfamiliar with any of these terms, they'll be covered later in the book.

---

[6] https://netbeans.org/
[7] http://www.zend.com/en/products/studio

Another perk is the built-in support for Zend Server—a special kind of server program used to run your PHP application and provide various analyses on running code and advanced debugging capabilities. Zend Server is a paid product, though, so if you want to use it in Zend Studio, you'll need to purchase a license. There's some basic information about Zend Server here: http://www.sitepoint.com/getting-know-zend-server-7/.

If your goal is to become the most "official" PHP developer you can be, with certificates and a total knowledge of officially endorsed tools and services, Zend Studio is right for you. Otherwise, I'd recommend either of PhpStorm or NetBeans.

Pros: great commercial support due to being owned by Zend; feature-rich, cross-platform, and integrates with other Zend products nicely

Cons: expensive, resource-intensive, and unstable; can be slow

Here are some other options you can research at your own leisure, a mix of commercial and free:

- Komodo IDE: http://komodoide.com/
- Eclipse with PDT: https://eclipse.org/pdt/
- Aptana Studio: http://www.aptana.com/
- phpDesigner: http://www.mpsoftware.dk/phpdesigner.php

There's also a list, ordered by popularity, at http://www.sitepoint.com/best-php-ide-2014-survey-results/.

Whichever IDE you choose, stick with it for at least a couple of months. The learning curve is often high, and you might feel overwhelmed by all the options when you first start using it. In time you'll become used to everything it offers, even if you'll only be using 10% of its functionality in your first 100 days of code. There's nothing wrong with switching IDEs at a later date, but give each one you try a reasonable chance.

At this point in time, it's unnecessary to download and install an IDE. This book is very light on code, and you'll only need one when we reach the later chapters.

Beware IDEs with WYSIWYG

One item IDEs do not and should not provide is WYSIWYG (What You See Is What You Get) editing. Dreamweaver, an IDE by Adobe, is one such tool. It's infamous for letting you get started easily because it allows you to pull in elements from a toolbar and drop them visually onto the screen, helping you "build code" as if playing with Lego blocks. Yet the code it generates is often suboptimal and bloated, containing more code than necessary and slowing a website down. What's more, by skipping the *real* coding part, you're effectively holding yourself back. You'll be unable to read anyone else's code, and you'll have a far tougher time learning to solve problems on your own.

Dreamweaver is not the only WYSIWYG editor, but it's by far the most popular one. If you run into an IDE that supports WYSIWYG, I wholeheartedly recommend you run in the opposite direction.

The Importance of Coding Standards

Coding standards are rules applied to code so that it's consistent across the entire project. For example, if Jim writes code this way:

```
if ($purchaseWasCompleted)
    $this->succeed();
else
    $this->error();
```

but Mike writes code like this:

```
($purchaseWasCompleted) ? $this->succeed() : $this->error();
```

and Joanna writes it as follows:

```
$pwc = $purchaseWasCompleted;
if ($pwc)
{
    $this->succeed();
```

```
} else {
    $this->error();
}
```

they have all written the same code differently. Now, if Jim reads through Mike's code, it might take him longer to go through it purely because he's used to his own way of writing. If they both examine Joanna's code, they'll be confused by the amount of code it took her to produce the same outcome as them in a different form.

If, however, they agree on a coding standard, they'll all produce the exact same code. Once they grow used to the standard, they'll be able to read each other's code more fluently, noticing bugs and reusing features with ease without any apparent language barriers.

Many IDEs have the ability to automatically apply certain coding standards; for example, the current favorite in the PHP world is the PSR-2 coding standard,[8] and all the IDEs mentioned have built-in mechanisms to at least check for it, if not apply it automatically and autocorrect your code. With PSR-2 (PSR stands for PHP Standard Recommendation), code such as this:[9]

```
class Test {
    protected $name;
    public function __construct($name) {
        $pointlessSum = 3+4;
        if ($name)
            $this->name = $name;
        else
            $this->name = "Default";
    }
    public function echoName() {
        echo $this->name;
    }
}
```

would be reformatted to look like this:

---

[8] http://www.php-fig.org/psr/psr-2/

[9] Don't worry if you don't understand this code, it's just for demonstration purposes.

```
class Test
{
    protected $name;

    public function __construct($name)
    {
        $pointlessSum = 3 + 4;
        if ($name) {
            $this->name = $name;
        } else {
            $this->name = "Default";
        }
    }

    public function echoName()
    {
        echo $this->name;
    }
}
```

Much more readable, isn't it? And all it took was some blank lines and spacing changes—that's more or less everything a coding standard does. Trivially simple, but vitally important. Standards also dictate other aspects, such as uppercase/lowercase letter conventions when naming classes and variables (notice the uppercase Test in the previously mentioned code); the position of curly braces in logic constructs such as if, for, and others; and more.

We strongly recommend using PSR-2. It's what the vast majority of high-quality projects out there use, making your coding style instantly compatible with that of many, many developers. It will also prepare you for reading their code fluently. With an IDE, this becomes incredibly easy. For example, in PhpStorm, you would go to **File > Settings > Editor > Code Style**, and select **PSR1/PSR2** (PSR-2 improves upon PSR-1, so this option applies both). Note that, depending on your version of PhpStorm, you *might* also have to select **Set From** in the **Code Style** windows. In other IDEs, it's as simple as googling for the phrase "PSR-2 in *EDITOR*" where *EDITOR* is your IDE of choice. It will yield a plethora of results.

The Command Line / Terminal

Finally, let's briefly look at the command line or terminal. First, a clarification on the terminology.

On Windows, the program you can see in Figure 2.3 is called the command prompt or command line:

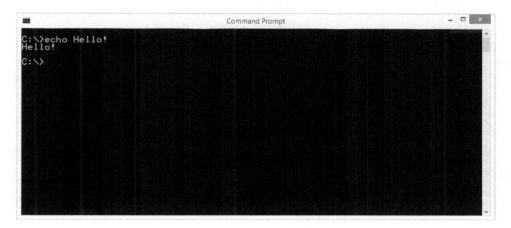

Figure 2.3. The Command Prompt says "Hello"

You run it by typing "cmd" or "command prompt" into the search box. In this, its most basic shape, it allows you to execute commands that run Windows programs, and either produce some written output (such as the `echo` command seen in Figure 2.3 that produces the output "Hello!"), or open applications you're already familiar with (if you type "notepad" into the command prompt and hit enter, the Notepad application will open). The command line has alternative implementations such as Cmder[10] (seen in Figure 2.4) or Console.[11] They are prettier versions that essentially perform the same task, but make certain actions such as copy pasting, tabbing interfaces, and selecting text simpler.

---

[10] http://bliker.github.io/cmder/
[11] http://sourceforge.net/projects/console/

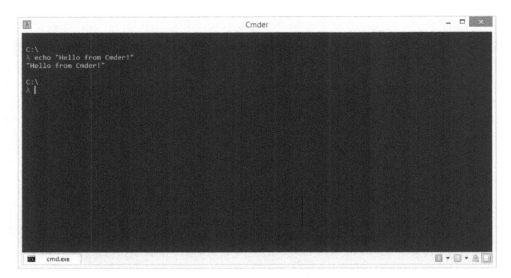

Figure 2.4. Cmder says "Hello"

On Mac and Linux machines, the program is called Terminal. To run it on either of these systems, open search and input "Terminal" and it should pop right up. It performs the same functions as the Windows Command Prompt, though has different commands. For example, the command to show the content of a directory (folder) in Windows is `dir` while on Apple and Linux it's `ls`.

Any developers worth their salt need to become friendly with the command line / terminal to maximize their potential. There are common workarounds to most command line commands and various shortcuts you can take at first, but it's never too long before those become more cumbersome and limiting instead of useful.

The differences between the Windows and the non-Windows versions are unimportant because you'll be using the Apple/Linux-specific commands, even on Windows. We'll show you how in Chapter 4.

The Community

As a final element of the programming environment, let's discuss asking for and providing help. The community around your programming language of choice is among the most important factors when learning to code. Being able to quickly and reliably obtain answers to problems you encounter can mean the difference between making or missing a deadline in a commercial project.

No developer knows the entire list of their preferred programming language's commands by heart. I've been programming in PHP for almost a decade, and I still regularly look up even the basic commands. Real knowledge lies not in knowing the commands by heart, but in knowing where to quickly find them.

That said, here are some resources you should bookmark in your browser right now under a folder titled "PHP Help."

PHP Mentoring

PHP Mentoring[12] aims to assist people in finding mentors and disciples. If you're an expert, you can mentor newbies, and if you're a beginner, you can find a mentor. A mentor will tell you about best practices, analyze your code and provide feedback, point out your mistakes, and set you on the right path whenever you stray. There are no fees associated with this; it's a purely voluntary effort by some good souls. If you're a total newbie, I suggest you apply for mentorship as soon as you flip this book's last page.

PHP.net Documentation

The official site of the programming language[13] is chock-full of code samples, with user comments further examining and explaining them. You will likely get little use out of it by just wandering through the pages aimlessly, but whenever you become stuck and need to check out a function or command, your first Google result will likely be PHP.net. If you're on a poor connection, or are often offline, there's also an offline version of these docs[14] that you can download stand-alone or as a Google Chrome application.[15]

Various Forums

The SitePoint forums[16] are an excellent resource with legions of people willing to help. You're almost guaranteed to receive an answer in minutes if you go into enough details with the question. The forums are gamified, meaning they have badges and points awarded to those who post there, encouraging the community to participate.

---

[12] http://phpmentoring.org/
[13] http://php.net
[14] http://php.net/download-docs.php
[15] http://bit.ly/phpdocs
[16] http://community.sitepoint.com

The StackExchange network is a consortium of context-specific (ranging from programming to chess and cooking) question-and-answer websites, made by the same people who built the software that powers the SitePoint forums. Being also gamified, this form of reward system entices users to participate more than usual, so one can gain an answer to a well-formed question in a matter of hours, if not minutes. There are three major subsites you should bookmark for the full experience:

- StackOverflow (http://stackoverflow.com/) is the most popular *generic* programming Q&A site. You can ask about any language here, as long as it's about development. You can also ask questions not dealing with programming directly, such as inquiries about IDEs, servers, and so on.

- Programming (http://programmers.stackexchange.com/) focuses solely on programming problems. If you get stuck coding, this is where you ask your questions, but make sure you google extensively first. Most of the newbie problems already have solutions online, and you won't be hard-pressed to find them.

- Code Review (http://codereview.stackexchange.com/) is used for having your code reviewed by other people and receiving feedback. It's important to accept feedback for what it is: apply the positive, brush off the negative, and learn from the constructive.

There are many other subsites in the network. Just look at the footer of any of these three—the full list is there. You might even find some that interest you outside of programming.

These resources listed will be of endless help to you at the beginning of your PHP journey. As soon as you feel even the least bit comfortable in basic PHP programming, I encourage you to seek out some intermediate and advanced tutorials by visiting SitePoint's PHP channel.[17]

Summary

In this chapter, we dealt with coding standards, code editors, communities, and other approaches that make coding more comfortable for ourselves, along with the people inheriting our code. Having a good coding *bon ton* from the get-go will pro-

---

[17] http://sitepoint.com/php

duce exponential improvements down the road as these helpful habits become muscle memory. Remember: good habits are just as difficult to break as bad ones!

3

The Application Environment

This chapter will focus on the application environment. We'll also discuss *AMP bundles such as XAMPP and why they're a poor choice; production /development parity; and performance and debugging.

If you're familiar with all these terms, feel free to skip this chapter.

Application Environments

The **application environment** is the term used to describe the environment your application can find itself in during various stages of its life cycle: the production environment, the development environment, and the staging environment.

The word **environment** refers to the hardware and software around your application; that is, everything used to power it.

Production

We'll start with the most straightforward of environments: the **production environment**.

When you **deploy** your application—in other words, upload it to a server and make it publicly accessible for the target audience—you're putting it *in production*, or *in use*. The production environment is your application's final destination, your code's purpose.

In an application's life cycle, the production environment is the **live server**—a server computer that's set up so that other people can connect to it and see your website. This live server will be configured to serve your application as efficiently as possible. All the extra files you used during development will be removed from the application via a process known as compiling or building, which is explained further on.

When in production, your site is considered to be live (or deployed) and will be accessible via its own domain; for example, `http://mysite.com`. When you launch your site (put it into production mode), you have cause for celebration, because this is the final step in your application's development process.

It is the equivalent of a chef cooking a meal in a restaurant and having it delivered to the patrons who ordered it.

Development

In the development environment, your application is being actively developed. The **development environment** is the computer you as the developer are using to develop the app, including the computers of all your team members, regardless of whether they are near you or remote. It is important to note that despite covering both aspects, the development environment refers more to *the state your app is in*, rather than its physical location—the app is in the state of *being developed*.

In the development environment, you have various tools at your disposal—from IDEs (see Chapter 2) to unit testing libraries and standards fixers, compilers and builders, file watchers, and more—anything you need to achieve the job at hand.

If we compare our application to a smartphone, the assembly plant it's being made in is the development environment. This environment contains all the necessary parts—the screen, the case, the battery, the various LEDs—and each part is individually tested before being used in the construction of a smartphone unit. This is called **unit testing**—ensuring each unit works.

For an example of unit testing in application development, see the section called "For Those Who Want More" at the end of this chapter.

To take the smartphone assembly analogy further, the battery being tested might require a separate charger attachment, or the screen may need to be tested using a robotic arm with synthetic fingers to ensure that the screen's touch sensitivity works.

Figure 3.1. Robot touching a smartphone screen

All these add-ons are there during development only. When converting from the development environment to the production environment (also known as *deploying*), these add-ons are removed. For our application, this means the aforementioned compilation/building step: various CSS and JavaScript files are merged together and shrunk so as to decrease the size of the website, making it appear faster when people visit it; unit tests are ignored and left behind in the development environment; and various other optimizations occur (covered later in the chapter)—all with the intention of making the final product maximize its appeal and potential when declared ready.

Hosts and Virtual Hosts

When you develop on your own computer, it's impossible to visit the URL `http://mysite.com` and expect to see your site; after all, your site is yet to go live—it's not on the Internet. To get around this and see our site as if it were live, we fake the Internet by defining virtual hosts.

Put simply, a **virtual host** gives an instruction to the server program installed on your computer, such as: IF a user requests `http://mysite.com` in the browser, run the file `mysite.php` through PHP and show its output in the browser.

As you can see, this is nearly identical to the regular request flow of live sites. But what makes the browser ask our own computer's server program for the `mysite.com` domain, rather than look it up on the Internet's name servers? The `hosts` file.

The `hosts` file is a special file present on every operating system. We mentioned it briefly in the section called "For Those Who Want More" in Chapter 1. It contains a list of domains and their appropriate IP addresses, so that any browser on your computer can read it and go directly to the IP address without having to talk to the DNS to check where to go. On Windows, that file is in `C:\Windows\System32\drivers\etc\hosts`, and on Linux and Mac machines it's in `/etc/hosts`. If you put an IP-name pair into this file, the computer will obey it. We can even try it out right now. Have no fear—there's nothing that can go wrong. Ready?

On Windows, enter the search field, type in "notepad" and once it appears, right-click it and select **Run as Administrator**. The system will then ask you for confirmation. In the window that opens, select **File > Open** and go to: **My Computer > C: > Windows > System32 > drivers > etc**. In the lower right corner of the Notepad window, you might need to select **All Files** so that the `hosts` file shows. Double-click to open it.

On Linux/Mac machines, open Terminal by searching for it. **On Linux**, open the default text editor as the administrator by typing `sudo gedit` into Terminal. You'll be asked for your administrator password. **On OS X**, enter `sudo /Applications/TextEdit.app/Contents/MacOS/TextEdit`, which will do the same task. In either of these editors, go to **File -> Open** and enter the directory `/etc` to find the `hosts` file. Double-click to open it.

Once the file is opened, note the first few lines: they'll all start with the hash symbol (#). This indicates that they're **comments**, and have no effect on the file. These serve to explain a file's purpose to the user, and they exist in PHP as well.

Now, under all these comment lines, add the following line:

```
208.117.229.217 bing.com
```

Save the file and open `http://bing.com` in your browser. You've just successfully redirected all requests to Microsoft's search engine Bing to Google! Of course, we don't want to keep these changes; feel free to delete this line or put a hash symbol in front of it to turn it into a comment, and save the file. You should be able to visit `http://bing.com` as normal again.

Using this method, we'll later redirect all browser requests for `http://mysite.com` (which will be our application's example domain) to our own computer's server. This will enable us to easily test the development version of our site without deploying it live.

Staging and Maintenance

The **staging environment** is a separate server (or several servers) containing a copy—also known as a mirror—of the production environment. The staging environment is often skipped in smaller companies or projects. It is designed to resemble the production environment as closely as possible, with matching versions of installed software, identical configuration values, and so on. Staging is for performing the final tests; for example, Facebook might redesign its front page, and before deploying it out into production for all users to see, it would deploy to its staging servers so that employees (dedicated non-programmers also known as the quality assurance team) can test everything first as if using it regularly. If everything goes well, the final deployment from staging to production happens.

Staging is beyond the scope of this book, but it's good to know about it. In the age of virtual machines and small throw-away projects, staging can be unnecessary, only coming into play with bigger long-term web applications.

There is also *maintenance mode*, a term we must cover in this context. It's a *mode* rather than an *environment* because the environment around the application doesn't change—only the status of the application does. It's usually just a switch on the production server telling those trying to access the website words to the effect of "Be right back, tuning up!"

The Evil of *AMP Bundles

When starting out in PHP development, it's tempting to download and install packages such as XAMPP,[1] WAMP,[2] MAMP,[3] or EasyPHP[4]. The AMP in those names stands for "Apache, MySQL, and PHP." XAMPP adds another P at the end for the Perl language. The first letter refers to the operating system: Windows, Linux, Mac OS X, or, in the case of XAMPP, cross-platform (meaning it works on any OS).

These bundles contain all the software you need to run your PHP applications quickly and easily on your computer. In one click, you can install everything you could ever need to write your very first PHP script. So, where's the evil in this?

- your computer will be polluted with unnecessary software
- you'll learn less than you would by installing manually
- testing is diffficult
- if you make a mistake, it's either very difficult or impossible to return to a previous state

Let's address these one by one.

Machine Pollution

Whenever you install software such as an *AMP stack on your computer, a chunk of your computer dies. Even if you delete the software later on, uncomfortable traces usually remain—often in the form of registry entries in Windows or file dust on Linux. In fact, this is especially apparent on Linux. While Windows and OS X applications are installed in an application folder with all related files inside it, on Linux the installation of software is like taking a shotgun to a castle built of Legos. One click and they're *everywhere*.

As time goes on, you'll install another library, another package, another tool. You'll keep adding supplementary software as you develop your app further, perhaps add

---

[1] https://www.apachefriends.org/index.html
[2] http://www.wampserver.com/en/
[3] http://www.mamp.info/en/
[4] http://www.easyphp.org/

different items entirely because you've started working on a new project in parallel. Maybe *app1* requires a PHP extension to edit images, and *app2* needs a PHP extension that allows it to package code into closed source archives, so that your code is hidden from your competition. In time, you'll have hundreds of megabytes of development software sitting on your machine, with no clue as to whether or not you still need it.

Your machine will slow down, applications will become less usable, and your development machine—the computer you're working on—will become so different from the production server you eventually intend to deploy your application on that you'll be unable to handle the difference gracefully. You'll end up regularly combating bugs on a live website and annoying your visitors to no end.

Learning is Progress, or How the Comfort of Your Comfort Zone is Overrated

By depending on these prebuilt packages, you also rob yourself of the experience of learning system administration work (**ops**, in short). Ops is, in larger companies, a team or person in charge of server issues—whether it be fixing bugs, installation of new software, upgrading existing software, and so on. In smaller teams or when working solo for clients, basic system administration is an essential skill to have.

While being able to install everything you need onto your computer with a single click is neat, there's no user interface on a server and thus nothing to click; you need to master the commands required to set up a server's software so that it can run your PHP application. Otherwise, you're either destined to hire a server administrator to help you out, or even worse, use shared hosting (a horror story that's explained in Chapter 6).

By refusing to rely on these *AMP bundles, you'll be forced to climb the learning curve of installing a server and other software by hand—knowledge that'll be useful in more ways than one if you're serious about this career path. Besides, nailing down the basics is really not that hard, as you'll see later in the book.

Testing

Say *app1* and *app2* are built on PHP 5.3, run MySQL 4.0, and are intended to go live on a server powered by Apache (the server software). Then, there's a new requirement: make sure *app1* works on PHP 5.6 and MySQL 5.1, and can be powered by Nginx (another server program that's competition to Apache, pronounced "engine x"). Uh-oh, what now?

We could update PHP to a newer version and check whether *app1* still works, but how do we then keep developing *app2* without accidentally using code that's unavailable in PHP 5.3 if our entire computer is now running 5.6? Likewise, we could upgrade MySQL to 5.1 and check that it still works, but how do we know MySQL didn't throw out some old features in version 5+ that would break app2 even if we fixed app1 to work on 5.1? After all, app2 still needs to work on 4.0 because it's probably still deployed on such a production server. Heck, how do we handle the Apache versus Nginx problem? Do we install both web servers on our computer and test for each? How do we switch them out? How do we ensure that we remember to test our site on one while the other is running?

And that's just for two apps. Now imagine if you had to deal with a dozen applications from ten different clients, each with different requirements. It all stops being fun very, very fast.

This separation of different software versions is easy to solve by means of virtual machines, which we'll talk about in Chapter 4.

The Uncleanable Mess

Finally, what if we try to install a new version of PHP, but something goes wrong? This scenario is especially common in OS X and Linux—now none of the PHP versions we have installed on the machine work and it's proving impossible to get a single site to run. What a mess! Instead of easily reverting to a previous running state, we're forced to spend the entire day debugging our own system and trying to make it run—not necessarily the right version, but just *run*.

Wouldn't it be great if we could just enter a command and have things go back to the way they were 10 minutes ago? Well, we can! This, too, will be demonstrated in Chapter 4.

Production/Development Parity

This complicated-sounding phrase is actually very simple—we've actually indirectly touched on it before. **Production/development parity** means nothing more than having the production and development environment as similar as possible to each other, preferably identical, so that anything you develop will automatically run in production without any excessive configuration or additional debugging or tweaking.

Achieving parity is very important for one's workflow due to the enormous amount of time it saves. Avoiding having to do any additional work for your application to run in production means having the freedom and time to focus on important business-related logic problems that actually benefit your application's context, rather than being stuck in a rut of constantly playing catch-up. Making a change in development and then having to make two changes in production for that change to become apparent is tedious at best and detrimental to a project's health at worst. You never know who on the team will slip up and cause the app to greet people with an error screen.

The best way to achieve parity is by having the exact same software running in your development environment as you do in your production environment. For example, if you're aiming to deploy your application to production onto a server running the Ubuntu Linux version 14.04 operating system, it's best that you develop on this operating system as well. However, what if we were running Windows, because we like to consume advanced multimedia content such as games, or we need powerful image and video manipulation software that just cannot exist on a Linux OS? Should we forsake all our other interests, install Linux over Windows, and strive for parity over anything else? Or should we just forsake parity and risk it while keeping our computer powerful, beautiful, and stable, sticking to our operating system of choice?

Fortunately, there's a third way that allows you to achieve the best of both worlds: virtual machines (covered in Chapter 4).

Performance and Debugging

The last aspects of the application environment we need to touch on is ensuring that the app is fast (performance) and bug-free (debugging). This section is entirely theoretical; it's just so you know what to expect later on when we come across some of these terms.

Performance is achieved through various methods of **optimization**. Contrary to the word's meaning, in application development optimization often has several layers and is rarely the change that immediately brings about the perfect solution. Performance includes, but is not limited to, several areas:

Optimizing the database

Often the slowest part of any website, the database can benefit from additional optimizations after it's been running for a while and the bottlenecks (the parts that are the slowest because they're unable to process the number of incoming requests fast enough) become apparent. Methods for database optimization include setting up indexes, splitting reads and writes, changing database engines, caching fetched data, and other mystical-sounding phrases.

Optimizing the front-end assets

We mentioned compilation and building earlier—it's how we optimize the website's front end. When a website is shown to users, they see output comprised of images, HTML, CSS, and JavaScript, all of which need to be downloaded and executed in the browser as explained in Chapter 1. The smaller these files are—and the fewer there are—the faster a website loads. Often, a website will have multiple CSS files and multiple JavaScript files. Combining each type into one bigger CSS or JavaScript file yields dramatic increases in a website's download speed. Another front-end asset optimization trick often done is serving images via a **content delivery network**, or CDN, a third-party service that hosts your images for you and ensures that the visitor to your website downloads them from a server closest to them, thereby further increasing speed. One can also reduce image size, create an **image sprite** by placing all images into one file, and more.

Optimizing the back end

This is also a compiling/building step. Test files are ignored, and files are merged into bigger ones to use instead of a million smaller ones. Some PHP applications are even compiled into another programming language such as C++, which is much, much faster.

Caching

Caching is saving previously needed files and responses for later, with the expectation of them being requested again. If you ask the database for the total number of users in your database, it will count them and give you the number. If you make it save this number for later (that is, cache it), next time it is asked it can just grab the already prepared information. When you ask the server "What do I get if I visit mysite.com/user/5?", it will tell you. If you tell it to remember the answer next time the question is asked, there's no need for the server to look as it already knows. Caching is so important in web development—there's a common saying that "cache is king." It can mean the difference between life and death for your application when a huge surge of traffic suddenly happens.

Debugging is tightly coupled with performance. Besides a nasty error screen for your users, a bug in the code can cause execution locks, holdups in your code where there should be none, repeated and unnecessary queries into your database, and more.

So, how does one measure performance or find bugs? There are many tools for **profiling** PHP applications (that's what finding bugs and measuring the performance of various aspects of your application is called). Two of the better ones are Z-Ray[5] and Blackfire[6] (we won't be covering them in this book as they are outside of its scope).

---

[5] http://www.zend.com/en/products/server/z-ray
[6] https://blackfire.io/getting-started

Beware Micro-optimization

It's important to note that a common newbie error is micro-optimizing. For example, it was once believed that using single quotes with strings (`$var = 'Some String'`) was faster than double quotes (`$var = "Some String"`). The performance gains such an optimization can bring to the table are negligent and almost always insignificant; instead, improving a complex SQL query or caching a remote HTTP call will always be an order of magnitude greater. When in doubt, use benchmarks and real data (such as those from Z-Ray or Blackfire), and never your gut.

Summary

In this chapter, we explored the application environment, covering the various ecosystems present around your application in a given phase of its life cycle. We talked about virtual hosts and configuring your computer to redirect website URLs to your own PHP installation rather than looking for results online, and we discussed the all-important development/production parity.

If it all seems overly complex, don't despair. This is only because we've dealt almost exclusively with theory so far—theory that is necessary to bravely proceed into the practical realm. In the following chapter, we'll get our hands dirty with some virtual machines.

For Those Who Want More

In the application universe, testing the individual components is referred to as **unit testing**—the testing of each individual set of code so that you know it works.

For example, a part of your application might have the ability to remove local symbols from every name and turn them into US-friendly letters. My last name "Škvorc" would thus be turned into "Skvorc." Turning Škvorc into Skvorc is a small set of code, or a **unit**. This unit is **testable**; that is, for any given input of "Škvorc" I expect an output of "Skvorc." I can then write a **unit test**, which is a file that defines the input and desired output, and when I run it, it tests whether or not this functionality still works. If, two months later, I change something in my application, I can easily run this test (which is still there) and check that this conversion still works. This sort of workflow ensures that you can upgrade your application later on without fear of breaking something you built before and forgot about. In our smartphone analogy at the beginning of the chapter, a single testable unit can be the touchscreen, or the battery.

Chapter 4

Virtual Machines

In this chapter, we're going to learn about virtualization and why it's absolutely essential for a quality development experience. We'll use industry-standard tools such as Vagrant, and talk about ways to make using virtual machines more user-friendly, so that they become more accessible to a wider audience.

I'd still advise reading this chapter even if you're familiar with virtualization, as it will undoubtedly contain information new to you. It will also explain and demonstrate the virtual box that we'll be using throughout the remainder of the book.

To use the tools we present in this chapter, you'll need to install some software on your computer. This software is cross-platform, so there's a version for your computer no matter which operating system you use.

Before proceeding, please ensure that you've installed the following:

- Vagrant, from https://www.vagrantup.com/

- VirtualBox, from https://www.virtualbox.org/

- Git, from http://git-scm.com/downloads

All these links include installation guides for every major operating system.

Virtual Machines Explained

Before we use virtual machines, or VMs, I'll explain what they are in general, and in the context of web development (which is not the same!).

What are VMs?

Your computer is a machine. It contains hardware such as the CPU, the GPU, some RAM, a hard drive, and so on. You need all this to run your operating system and the apps installed into it. A **virtual machine** is a special type of application that reserves a part of your computer and pretends it's a real machine on its own. For example, a virtual machine might reserve a part of your CPU and 2GB of RAM from your main machine, along with 20GB of hard-drive space. These resources are then brought together into a whole, seen in Figure 4.1, which can act as a computer on its own. It can have its own operating system independent from the main machine's OS (the **host**) with its own applications installed.

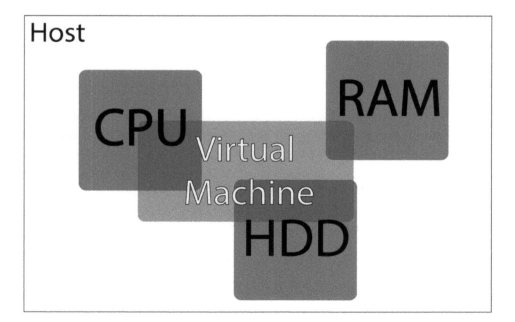

Figure 4.1. Visualizing a virtual machine

The operating systems—in fact, the entire environments of the different machines (the host and the virtual machine running on the host)—are entirely independent and, indeed, unaware of each other. The host knows it has fewer resources at its disposal, but is unconcerned. The virtual machine knows it has some resources at its disposal, but has no idea they're not real; it *thinks* they're actual hardware parts.

A virtual machine is, quite literally, a computer within a computer. Some people use them for running video games on operating systems without native support for them; for example, running Windows games on a Linux system. Security companies use them as **sandboxes**, environments in which they can let loose a virus or potentially malicious piece of code without worrying about the consequences: if the virtual machine gets damaged, it's rebuilt with two simple commands (it's virtual, after all!). Enterprise companies use them as a way to avoid updating their software. Rather than spend billions on a software rewrite because their internal application depends on Windows XP and the newest version is Windows 10, they'll spend much less on buying Windows XP licenses and running Windows XP virtual machines inside of their Windows 10 host machines, enabling their app to live longer while enjoying the increased security of a newer host operating system.

In development, a virtual machine is used as an isolated environment for your application. You can install different versions of PHP and MySQL in it, and you can break anything as a virtual machine can be reset into its original state easily. This is what makes virtual machines very appealing, not only for testing code on different versions of PHP on different operating systems, but also for development/production parity (discussed in the Chapter 3): it allows you to configure a virtual machine to resemble a live server as closely as possible, thus being able to test the code as if it was online, minimizing errors.

Getting to Know VirtualBox and Vagrant

VirtualBox, one of the pieces of software we installed in the introduction to this chapter, is used to *build* these virtual machines. It takes the resources from the host, and gives them to the virtual machine. It is what boots up the virtual machine (they need booting up just like regular machines), helping it live out its illusion of reality. VirtualBox has many features including, but not limited to, the sharing of graphics cards (enabling a virtual display within your display), inputs (keyboards, mice, and so on), and sound (playing sound from the virtual machine on the host's speakers). Figure 4.2 depicts VirtualBox in action.

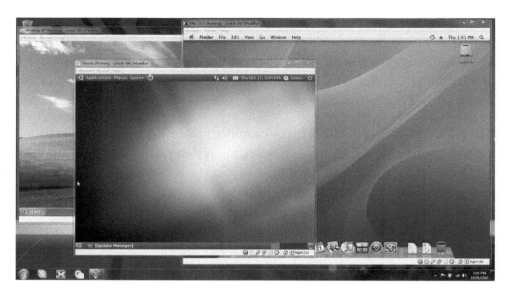

Figure 4.2. VirtualBox in action

However, this can be very resource-consuming and can be incredibly sluggish. Booting up virtual machines with full graphic interfaces takes just as long as booting up on old hardware matching the hosts's power of the reserved resources; consequently, this would be unnecessarily slow when developing for the Web. Furthermore, most web developers have their favorite IDE and browser, along with other tools, all configured for a pleasant workflow. If developers had to reinstall and reconfigure these tools into every new virtual machine they booted up, their profession would rapidly lose its appeal. Developers want to be able to use the tools they know and love without much configuring; they want to be able to dive into a new project as soon as possible, so they want to keep their tools on the host.

This is where Vagrant comes in. Vagrant is a helper tool that uses VirtualBox to create "headless VMs." In other words, it boots them up without the multimedia angle (that is, without graphics and sound) so that they look almost like actual servers; all you are given is a terminal application, as seen in Figure 4.3.

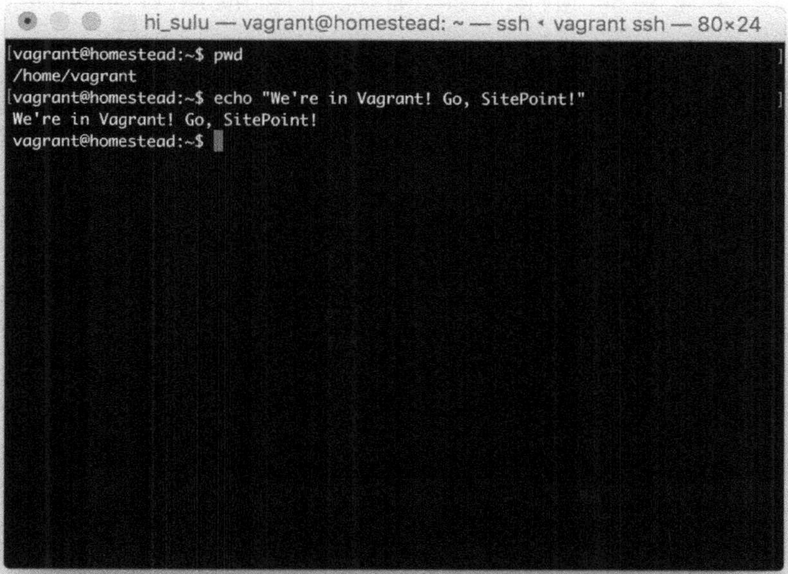

Figure 4.3. Vagrant in action

We'll discuss Vagrant in more depth below.

The Benefits of VMs

To recap, the benefits of using VMs in development are:

- they're easy to destroy and rebuild into an initial state without any consequences

- you can use your favorite applications on your host machine

- you can achieve development/production parity by configuring a VM to be similar to your live server, thus enjoying a more bug-free deployment

- you get to learn some system administration

- it's impossible to do any harm to your host machine when using VMs as they're completely isolated

▨ it's easy to share entire configurations with other people (by sending them a Vagrantfile—more on this later) so that they have the *exact same setup* on their machine

▨ there's no need to install PHP, servers, and databases on your host machine, thus keeping your main operating system clean and fast indefinitely

Vagrant in a Nutshell

Vagrant is an application that uses another application (in our case, VirtualBox) to create virtual machines via simple commands such as `vagrant up`. Where punching in such commands would usually be tedious, error-prone, and incredibly time-consuming (albeit possible!) in a VirtualBox-only world, Vagrant helps us shorten the process to be up and running incredibly quickly.

Vagrant knows what it needs to do with the help of a specific Vagrantfile, which contains all the instructions for how to set up the environment, making the process of creating a new *virtual box* much simpler.

Vagrant Boxes

Take, for example, your own computer. It has a plethora of installed applications and services, and probably a bunch of media in your home folder such as pictures, music, and so on. If you had the ability to package your entire machine's collection of software into a single file, so that when unpacked on another computer it turns out a clone of your own machine, you would be building a box. This is what **Vagrant boxes** are: preconfigured Virtual machine shells with some pre-installed software (provisioned software—covered in the next section), making it easy to dive right into a project.

All the various Vagrant boxes can be found on https://atlas.hashicorp.com/boxes/search. These are boxes preconfigured by other people and available to everyone for free. You can find anything from bare-bones operating system installations to fully configured environments that are compatible with specific software. You can use these preconfigured boxes, tweak existing ones, or build your own. For resources on this, please see the links at the end of this chapter.

Provisioning

A **provisioner** is a tool used to automatically install some prerequisite software onto a machine (whether virtual or not). Provisioners are often used in real live servers as well to bring them up to par with the requirements of the application being deployed. Some popular provisioners are Ansible,[1] Puppet,[2] and Chef.[3] A provisioner accepts a **recipe**, a list of steps required to prepare an environment for an application.

For example, assuming we're about to build a PHP application, we might have a provisioner do the following for us on a bare-bones Vagrant box:

- install Git
- install PHP
- install some PHP extensions
- install MySQL
- set the default MySQL username and password
- download sample database data and import it into MySQL

Doing all this manually is tedious and error-prone. Provisioners have the awesome ability of taking care of operating system differences for us so they can be run on our virtual machine, live server, staging server, and so on. They always perform the same operations and produce the same result: the prerequisites to run our application will be taken care of for us.

Vagrant integrates closely with the various provisioners and employs them to set up the environments we tell it to set up. Thus, when booting up a Vagrant box the virtual machine is started up first, followed by the designated provisioner. There's no need to know about provisioners at this point, but there will be links to some more resources about them at the end of this chapter. We'll be using a preconfigured Vagrantfile for our experiments in this chapter, along with an already preconfigured provisioning script, in order to keep matters simple and newbie-friendly.

---

[1] http://www.ansible.com/
[2] https://puppetlabs.com/
[3] https://www.chef.io/chef/

Another approach to easy provisioning is using various available graphical user interfaces (GUIs) to build your own Vagrantfile (and thus, provisioning script), such as by using PuPHPet[4], as shown in Figure 4.4..

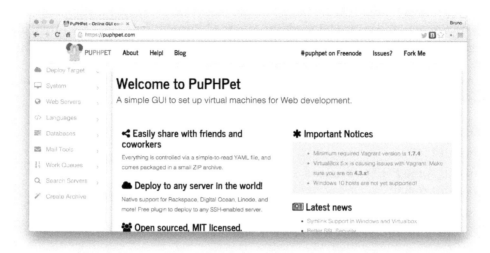

Figure 4.4. Provisioning with PuPHPetPu

PuPHPet (which uses Puppet as a provisioner), and Phansible[5] (which uses the arguably simpler Ansible as a provisioner) are good examples of GUIs for setting up virtual machines. These GUIs will enable you to go through a step-by-step process of selecting all the software and configuration values you need for your environment, ultimately producing a Vagrantfile, with which you can easily boot up your desired environment. If you'd like to see an example of this, there's a great post about PuPHPet on SitePoint.[6]

Using Vagrant

Enough theory, let's try and use Vagrant by setting up a version of Homestead, which is a preconfigured virtual machine, and then I'll explain it all in the next section. Assuming you've installed the software from the introduction part of this chapter, please go to the URL https://github.com/Swader/homestead_improved. Once there, click the **Download Zip** button shown in Figure 4.5.

---

[4] http://puphpet.com
[5] http://phansible.com/
[6] http://www.sitepoint.com/build-virtual-machines-easily-puphpet/

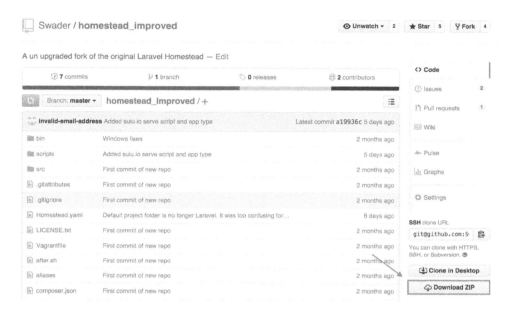

Figure 4.5. Downloading Homestead

Download the file somewhere onto your computer (I recommend your home folder) and unzip it, either by double-clicking or by right-clicking and selecting **Extract here**.

Now it's time to fire up our old friend Terminal, or command line, again. On OS X or Linux, open the Terminal app. On Windows, because we installed Git at the beginning of this chapter, run the program Git Bash as it should now be available.

Then, let's enter the folder into which we extracted the contents of the **homestead_improved-master.zip** archive, seen in Figure 4.6. The command should be as simple as `cd ~/homestead_improved-master`, assuming you unzipped into the home folder.

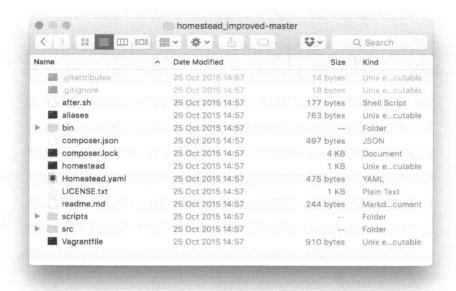

Figure 4.6. The folder upon being unzipped

Now that you're inside the **homestead_improved-master** folder, run the command `bin/folderfix.sh`. Then, run the command `vagrant up`.

This will download the box and place it in a common location, so it doesn't have to be downloaded again when you make other "homesteads" in the future. It will then use the box to create the virtual machine by following instructions in the Vagrantfile. Depending on whether you've done this before, downloading the box might take a while.

While waiting, add the following entry to your `hosts` file (see the Hosts and Virtual Hosts section of Chapter 3 chapter for details on how and why to do this):

```
192.168.10.10 homestead.app
```

Once the original Terminal window where you ran the `vagrant up` command is done and waiting for more input, open your browser and visit the URL: `http://homestead.app/`. The screen should read `No input file specified`. If it does, everything works! Now in the `homestead_improved-master` folder, make a subfolder called **Project**. Inside it, create another called **public**. Finally, in that folder create a file called **index.php** with the following content inside:

```php
<?php

echo "Hello Virtual Machine!";
```

Reload the `http://homestead.app/` URL in your browser, and the screen should read "Hello Virtual Machine!"

Let's now examine everything that happened.

Homestead Improved: Explanation

When we visited the URL `https://github.com/Swader/homestead_improved`, we went to GitHub, a coding social network for open-source projects. Homestead is a preconfigured virtual machine running the Ubuntu operating system with critical system security patches installed and some commonly used software for PHP development; that is, a new version of PHP and some databases, among others. Homestead Improved is a slightly enhanced version of Homestead that makes it even easier to get started with some things. Every project on GitHub is a **repository**, a set of files.

The Homestead Improved repository contains all the files necessary to run a Vagrant environment, specifically the Vagrantfile. This Vagrantfile loads the contents of all the other important files in the repository and uses the combination of these files to set up (provision) your environment. This is what the `vagrant up` command was for: reading the Vagrantfile and following instructions within.

When we ran the `folderfix` command, we executed a **shell script**, which is a tiny program whose sole purpose is to establish the folder from which it's being run and set that folder up as shared with the VM. Remember that VMs are isolated environments unaware of the host machine they're running on? If they're completely unconnected, how can we then use our host machine's applications to write code that runs in the VMs? The answer is folder sharing. By *mapping* a specific location on our host machine (the current folder) to a specific location within the VM (the **Code** folder), we tell Vagrant to copy every file we create or change in this folder into the designated location inside the VM. This creates a weak link between the host and the virtual machine, enabling files to be shared; this, in turn, allows us to use the

IDEs installed on the host machine to write code that eventually runs on the virtual machine.

So, what about that `No input file specified` message? If you look at **Homestead.yaml** in the `sites` block, you see the following:

```
sites:
    - map: homestead.app
      to: /home/vagrant/Code/Project/public
```

This means that whenever we try to visit `http://homestead.app`, the computer should look for files to run inside the path in the `to` line. But since a fresh Homestead Improved VM is yet to have any files in that location, the message we receive is one of a missing input file. We then fix this by putting an **index.php** file in that location, giving us our "Hello Virtual Machine" message.

Defining New Sites

Most of the time, you'll want a custom folder path and site URL for your project. Let's define a new one on the same Homestead Improved VM we just used. A single VM can host an unlimited number of apps/projects; it's up to you to decide how you want to distribute them across various machines/environments for testing or development isolation purposes.

Open the file **Homestead.yaml** again. Under `sites`, add another `map` / `to` pair. Make sure the indentation matches the pair above it, as they need to have the same padding—that's a rule of the YAML file format. I'll make a new site called **test.app** so that my `sites` block looks as follows:

```
sites:
    - map: homestead.app
      to: /home/vagrant/Code/Project/public
    - map: test.app
      to: /home/vagrant/Code/test
```

This means: look for the files of the `test.app` URL in the folder **/home/vagrant/Code/test**.

Now make a new **test** folder in the **homestead_improved-master** folder, and inside it put the file **index.php** with the contents:

```
<?php

echo "Hello ".(isset($_GET['name']) ? $_GET['name'] : "World")."!";
```

Then add 192.168.10.10 test.app to your **hosts** file.

To apply these changes, the VM needs to reload the configuration. We handle this by executing the command vagrant provision from the command line inside the homestead_improved-master folder.

If you now visit http://test.app/ in the browser, you should see "Hello World!" And if you visit http://test.app?name=Vagrant, you should see "Hello Vagrant!", as shown in Figure 4.7. You've just done some PHP programming in a virtual machine!

Figure 4.7. Our first program in a virtual machine

You probably noticed that a new site requires you to add a new sites block, but not a new folders entry. This is because we've set up Homestead Improved in such a way that its entire master folder (the one you're in: **homestead_improved-master**) is shared into the **Code** folder of the VM, so any subfolders of these two folders are automatically shared and kept in synchronization with each other as well. Technically, we could define separate folder mappings that go outside the

homestead_improved-master folder and share a completely arbitrary location from outside of it with a completely arbitrary location inside the VM, but it is my feeling that adopting this isolated approach keeps it much cleaner.

Shutdown

The VM, while running, takes up a significant share of your host machine's resources. In fact, if you look at **Homestead.yaml**, you'll notice that it takes one CPU core and two entire gigabytes of RAM (lines two and three in the file). Leaving a VM on while not in use is wasteful and slows down your host computer, so powering it down (just like shutting a computer down when you leave the house, for example) makes sense. We do this by executing the `vagrant halt` command from the terminal while inside the **homestead_improved-master** folder. Alternatively, the `vagrant suspend` command can be used—it's faster, but ends up eating a bit more hard drive space, even while off.

Let's halt the machine. Inside the **homestead_improved-master** folder, run:

```
vagrant halt
```

To completely destroy the VM, wiping its hard drive and all the software installed after download, we can execute `vagrant destroy`. To revive it and reinitiate the provisioning process, we can run `vagrant up` again and all will be as it was. This is the beauty of Vagrant—destroying and rebuilding is only two commands away, lending itself perfectly to experimentation with even the most volatile cutting-edge technologies.

Further Reading

This is, more or less, everything you need to know about Vagrant and VMs to get started properly. Homestead is, of course, a shortcut—but it's a good one worth starting with. Once you're comfortable with it, feel free to explore other approaches such as building a box from scratch, modifying a Vagrantfile, using a different base box to boot up a different operating system, and more.

For further reading and more in-depth information, please see the following articles:

- Re-introducing Vagrant: The Right Way to Start with PHP[7]

- Quick Tip: Get a Homestead Vagrant VM Up and Running[8]

- How to Create and Share a Vagrant Base Box[9]

- Vagrantfile Explained: Setting Up and Provisioning with Shell[10]

Summary

In this chapter, we learned about virtualization—a crucial part of anyone's development workflow, even if they're yet to know it. We introduced Vagrant, and added new sites to a preconfigured Vagrantfile setup called Homestead Improved. We also explained why one should always use virtual machines while developing, even for the simplest projects.

In the next chapter, we'll talk about version control and why it's essential for any kind of progressive work.

---

[7] http://www.sitepoint.com/re-introducing-vagrant-right-way-start-php/

[8] http://www.sitepoint.com/quick-tip-get-homestead-vagrant-vm-running/

[9] http://www.sitepoint.com/create-share-vagrant-base-box/

[10] http://www.sitepoint.com/vagrantfile-explained-setting-provisioning-shell/

5

Versioning Systems

In this chapter, we'll cover versioning systems. In particular, we'll be talking about Git and GitHub, as those are by far the most popular two tools in use as far as versioning and code sharing are concerned.

If you're an active user of Git and/or GitHub and are familiar with both the importance and use of versioning systems in general, feel free to skip this chapter. Otherwise, I strongly advise you to read it as it's easy to absorb, and absolutely essential in your future work.

If you didn't read the previous chapter—though it is recommended that you do, so please don't skip it—install the following tools before proceeding:

- Vagrant, from https://www.vagrantup.com/

- VirtualBox, from https://www.virtualbox.org/

- Git, from http://git-scm.com/downloads

Versioning Basics

In software development, the term **versioning** or, more accurately, **version control** refers specifically to the ability to:

- track the changes of files over time and label those changes with helpful change messages

- revert those files to any of their previous versions (an infinite number of "undo" operations)

- share those changes with others in a way that's visible and immediately clear to every team member

- enable more than one person to edit the same file at the same time, and being able to sync those changes

- have a central location for all source code from which all other team members (and sometimes random enthusiasts) can grab your code and work on it

Conceptually, version control in software development is similar to applying version control in other programs, such as tracking people's contributions in Google Docs documents, using the undo operation in Photoshop, and so on.

While version control is important in any kind of development, it is especially precious in teamwork. In the past, teams working on the same codebase would share code snippets over email (so-called "patchbombs"), which required a lot of manual synchronization and administrative overhead in accepting changes and updates.

With tools such as Git and GitHub, this changed.

Git and GitHub

Git is an application for version control, or what is generally called a version control system (VCS). It handles all the points listed under what constitutes versioning, and more. **GitHub** is a variety of social network for coding, powered by Git.

Git

Git is a command-line application that's generally without a GUI. It's used strictly from the terminal or from within Git Bash, a tool that becomes automatically available on Windows when you install Git.

Helper tools with graphical user interfaces do exist—partially removing the need for manually punching in commands—but in the vast majority of use cases we require a version of the terminal. From now on in this book, whenever there's an instruction like "execute the command `git push`", it's assumed we are using the terminal or Git Bash to enter the command.

Through Git, we can easily download repositories such as Homestead Improved from the last chapter without having to use the **Download** button. Instead, we use a command called `clone`, like so:

```
git clone https://github.com/swader/homestead_improved
```

Notice that we used GitHub in the URL. We'll explain that in the GitHub section shortly.

How does it work?

In a nutshell, Git uses a hidden **.git** folder inside your project's folder to track all the changes and previous versions of the files. Whenever you make a new **commit** (that's a specifically flagged point in time when something changed in a given file or set of files), Git will store a copy of the old version and new version in the **.git** folder so that we can later refer to them if needed. That way, if we need to undo a change, we just tell Git to reset to a previous point in time with, for example, `git reset 47298720dbf`, where the code at the end is the name or flag of the commit. We'll link to a more comprehensive Git guide at the end of this chapter. Reading it will make you a Git master within a day or two, tops.

Alternatives

Git is far from being the only VCS. There are others such as Mercurial,[1] SVN,[2] CVS,[3] and many, many more, but Git is the most widely used one. It is *the* VCS to use if you want to contribute to open-source projects today, as the vast majority of them use it. It is also what mostly powers GitHub, so you'll be part of the pack from the get-go.

GitHub

When using Git, you have the ability to `clone` repositories from any remote endpoint, provided the code is there. For example, if I have some source code and I put it on a live server (one accessible to the Internet), then configure this server to accept remote Git calls, anyone who has Git installed can clone this source code by running:

```
git clone https://myserver/myrepo.git
```

However, not everyone has the time, money, know-how, or patience to set up a server just to host code for others to access. This is where GitHub comes in.[4]

GitHub is a website on which people can host their repositories for free, but there's a catch—all repositories are immediately accessible to everyone. They're public. Private repositories are supported, but cost money. This is ideal when developing projects for clients that should be kept private—especially from the client's competition. For free private repos, there are alternative websites such as GitLab[5] and Bitbucket,[6] but those aren't nearly as popular as GitHub, hence why we'll use GitHub in this book. In your own adventures, feel free to use any service you like.

But why would one even want to use a service such as GitHub for their code? Apart from the obvious answer of being able to share your code with others easily and for free, services such as GitHub can be lifesavers when your machine dies and you lose all its content. If you regularly **pushed** (a Git term for "upload") to the repository's **remote** origin—meaning its GitHub URL—you're safe from disaster: your entire

---

[1] https://www.mercurial-scm.org/
[2] https://subversion.apache.org/
[3] http://www.nongnu.org/cvs/
[4] https://github.com
[5] https://gitlab.com
[6] https://bitbucket.com

file history is preserved and you can continue where you left off on another computer. Furthermore, many other companion services exist that integrate automatically with GitHub. One example would be Travis CI,[7] a service that runs checks on the code to make sure it all still works whenever changes to a GitHub repository are detected. If something is wrong, Travis notifies you via email and updates a little badge on the repo's main web page warning users about the latest version.

Now that we've covered the theory of Git and GitHub, how about seeing it in action?

Git in Action

Let's learn using a practical example. I recommend (and will assume) you put your projects into your home folder, the path for which the shortcut is ~. If you opt to use a different one, please adapt the code that follows.

Preparing the Environment

As we've done in previous chapters, we first need to configure a VM in which we'll do our experiments. We *could* do all this on our host machine, but remember that the end goal is to keep the host machine as clean as possible, all while using a fully discardable and experiment-friendly environment for all the playing around we can think of. Here's what to do:

1. Open Git Bash on Windows or Terminal on OS X/Linux.

2. Go into your home folder by executing the command `cd ~`.

3. Clone the **homestead_improved** repository into a folder named `hi_phpenv` with the command: `git clone https://github.com/swader/homestead_improved hi_phpenv`. You've just learned about `git clone`!

4. Enter the newly made folder with `cd hi_phpenv`.

5. Execute `bin/folderfix.sh`

6. Open **Homestead.yaml** and change the `sites` block so that it looks like this:

---

[7] https://travis-ci.org/

```
sites:
    - map: phpenv.app
      to: /home/vagrant/Code/phpenv
```

7. Add a new `hosts` entry:

```
192.168.10.10 phpenv.app
```

If you're unfamiliar with this step, please see the section Hosts and Virtual Hosts in Chapter 3.

8. Finally, run `vagrant up` in the **hi_phpenv** folder. This will boot up the VM, and you should be able to access `http://phpenv.app/` in your browser and see the message `No input file specified`.

This is a procedure you'll have to repeat with every new project. After all, every project deserves a fresh environment, oblivious to the mistakes and changes of the last one. But fear not, in due time the procedure will become muscle memory, and you'll get from start to finish in a minute flat. To save you from having to remember the procedure or continuously refer to this chapter, you can find a helpful guide at http://www.sitepoint.com/quick-tip-get-homestead-vagrant-vm-running/.

Creating a "Hello World" page

With our environment ready, the path to learning about Git and GitHub is clear:

1. In the **hi_phpenv** folder, create a new folder named `phpenv`. You can do this either through your host machine's file explorer or via the Terminal / Git Bash with `mkdir phpenv`. Change into the directory with `cd phpenv`.

2. Make a new file called **index.php** and give it the contents:

```
<?php echo "Hello World";
```

3. Try visiting `http://phpenv.app/` in the browser to make sure it works.

We now have our "Hello World" page. We're proud of our code and want to share it with the world. Let's use Git and GitHub to do that.

Git

Before we put anything on GitHub, we'll tell Git to turn our source code into a repository.

Repo Initialization

▨ While in the **phpenv** folder (that's **hi_phpenv/phpenv**), run `git init`. This is an initialization command that will create an empty **.git** folder. It is hidden by default, but you can see it if you execute `ls -a`.

▨ When developing with the power of a version control system such as Git, you might want to ensure certain files are never added to a repository. For example, if you had a database password in a configuration file, it would be unwise to let this file be accessible online, as it would leak your password to everyone looking at your repo. For this purpose, **ignore files** exist. These are special files for Git with the filename being **.gitignore** and contents that list files to ignore line-by-line, like so:

```
mypassword.php
sensitive-folder/*
```

This piece of code will make sure the file `mypassword.php` and everything inside the folder `sensitive-folder` is never added to a repository, nor ends up in anyone else's clone of your code.

If you're using an IDE to write this code, and I hope you are (see Chapter 2), you'll find that it likes to put its own helper files into the project's root. For example, PhpStorm loves to make an `.idea` folder and place some configuration values inside that pertain to the current project. I definitely want to avoid having anyone who clones my code be forced to also copy my IDE configuration, so let's use an ignore file to prevent this.

Create a **.gitignore** file in the folder with the command `touch .gitignore`, or from within your IDE. Then edit it and give it the contents of the file at https://gist.github.com/Swader/7844111 , which is an ignore file that takes into account all the various IDE and OS configurations you can run into when working on PHP projects.

Another way of making sure you never have to add this to a project's `.gitignore` file again is by adding it to your global **.gitignore**. To see how, check out this handy guide from GitHub: https://help.github.com/articles/ignoring-files/.

With both our code and our **.gitignore** file ready, we'll need a readme file. A **readme** file is the first file a GitHub repo displays to visitors, so it's good to include some useful information about the author, the purpose of the code, ways to use it, ways to contribute to it, and so on. Make a **README.md** file in the `phpenv` folder via your IDE or the Terminal with **touch README.md** and give it some content such as:

```
# Hello World

This is a README file from the Jump Start PHP Environment book.
Learning about Git and GitHub!
```

The **.md** extension indicates that this is a Markdown[8] (MD) file—one type of file GitHub uses to display the readme content in a pretty, formatted manner. Knowing MD isn't necessary in order to understand the rest of the content in this book; however, it is important in coding life, so I recommend you take a look at https://guides.github.com/features/mastering-markdown when you find the time.

Adding and Committing

To add all the files in our project to our repository, execute `git add -A`. The `add` command tells Git to add any changes that were made to the repo's history track. The `-A` flag means "add new files, add changes to existing files, and add file deletions (that is, make note of all the files that were removed)".

What this actually did, though, was merely tell that Git we'll be tracking the changes to all the files it just added *some time in the future*. To actually make a commit, and by that create a restorable point in our project's life cycle, we need to use the `commit` command: `git commit -m 'Added my first files!'`. The `-m` means "commit message" and it's where you label your changes. Anyone coming into your project will be able to look at that exact point in time and see your message, instantly knowing why you did what you did. Execute this now.

---

[8] https://help.github.com/articles/github-flavored-markdown/

Now that our files are added and committed, let's introduce a change. Open **index.php** again and change "Hello World" to "Hello Bob" so that the file looks like this:

```
<?php echo "Hello Bob";
```

Then make another add and commit: first `git add -A`, then `git commit -m 'Changed World to Bob'`.

Visit the page in the browser again via `http://phpenv.app/` and notice how it now says "Hello Bob."

Reset

We really like Bob, but our boss doesn't, and asks us to change it back to "World." We could make a change and commit, and be done with it. But in complex projects with many files, reverting changes by manually changing files back to the state they were in before will just fail to work. That's why we have the `reset` command. To reset back to the previous commit, we need to find out the ID of that commit.

We can do this with:

```
git log
```

In my case, as you can see in Figure 5.1, the ID of the commit before the most recent one is b6adf1756bb9b94fcf9b46c6121180dc12b96176.

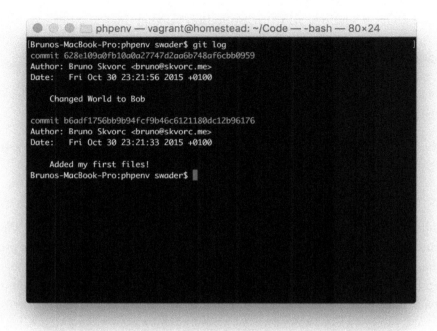

Figure 5.1. Finding the ID of our commit

To reset to it, we execute:

```
git reset --hard b6adf1756bb9b94f
```

Notice how we used a shorter hash than what `git log` gave us. That's a feature of Git—just the first ten or so characters of a hash are enough to identify the correct commit we're looking for.

Our entire Bob modification is removed and it's as if nothing ever happened. A refresh of `http://phpenv.app` will confirm this.

It can be tedious to find out the exact commit ID, so shorthand identifiers such as `HEAD~1` are supported, too. `HEAD` is "current commit" and `~1` tells Git to go one parent into the past. Doing `git reset --hard HEAD~1` would have worked, too.

The --hard option tells Git "no matter what changes we have pending, this reset is more important than anything, so just do it—no questions asked." Without --hard, Git would have complained if we had made any other uncommitted changes.

GitHub

Now that we're happy with our source code again, let's put it online for others to clone and inspect. Sign up for a GitHub account if you haven't already, at https://github.com.

1. In the top-right corner, click the **Create New > New repository** button, shown in Figure 5.2.

Figure 5.2. Creating a new repository

2. Give it a name of your choice, such as "phpenv," and leave all other options on their default value.

3. On the next screen, you're given instructions on how to place some existing code online, seen in Figure 5.3.

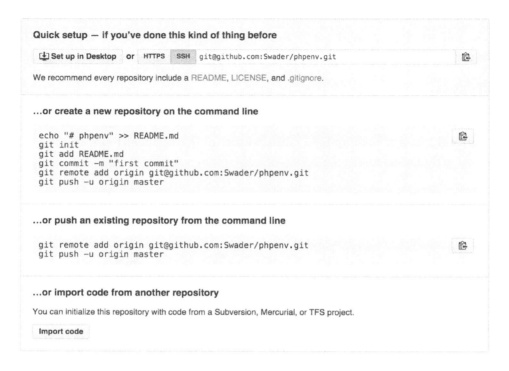

Figure 5.3. Instructions on adding code to the repository

Let's follow these instructions, and in our Terminal/Git Bash execute (don't forget to modify USERNAME in the URL to match yours, of course):

```
git remote add origin git@github.com:USERNAME/phpenv.git
git push -u origin master
```

The `remote add` command tells Git "this repository has a copy that isn't on this machine. The copy's URL is this, and we can refer to it as 'origin' in the future." The `push` command tells Git to "upload all the changes we've made so far to the URL you know as 'origin'." The `-u` flag allows you to just say `git push` in the future, without `origin master`, but needs to be specified during the first run. `master` refers to the branch name, but diving into branches is outside the scope of this book for now (see the section called "Useful Resources" at the end of the chapter for more information). The output produced by these commands should resemble the following:

```
Counting objects: 5, done.
Delta compression using up to 8 threads.
Compressing objects: 100% (4/4), done.
Writing objects: 100% (5/5), 713 bytes | 0 bytes/s, done.
Total 5 (delta 0), reused 0 (delta 0)
To git@github.com:Swader/phpenv.git
 * [new branch]      master -> master
Branch master set up to track remote branch master from origin.
```

4. Visit the URL of your repository in your GitHub account, and you should see the files you created residing there, as depicted in Figure 5.4.

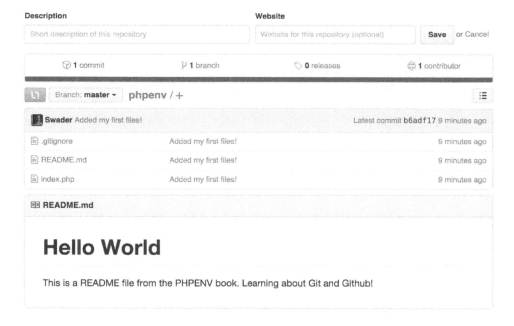

Figure 5.4. Our files are now in the repository

To share this code with others, send them the link. They can then use the `git clone` command to clone it to their computers, or download it as a zip archive as we did in the previous chapter.

Finally, let's add one more change and push it to the GitHub repo for all to see.

Modify the **index.php** file so it contains the following:

```php
<?php

echo "Hello ".(isset($_GET['name']) ? $_GET['name'] : "World");
```

This code, when run with PHP, allows the visitor to input their name like this `http://phpenv.app?name=Bob` and see the message "Hello Bob." Go ahead and test it out.

Now let's add and commit:

```
git add -A
git commit -m 'Name is now dynamic!'
```

 Be Careful with Quotes

If you receive a warning saying `-bash: !": event not found`, it's because you're using double (`"`) rather than single quotes (`'`). Make sure that you use single quotes with your commit messsage.

Finally, let's push the code:

```
git push
```

If we now refresh the GitHub page, we should see the updated state of our code as shown in Figure 5.5.

Branch: **master** ▾ **phpenv** / +		☰
Swader My name is now dynamic!		Latest commit dcf548a a minute ago
📄 .gitignore	Added my first files!	13 minutes ago
📄 README.md	Added my first files!	13 minutes ago
📄 index.php	My name is now dynamic!	a minute ago

Figure 5.5. The updated repository

Notice how the commit message next to **index.php** is different from the others? This indicates that it's the only file that changed in the latest commit.

Go and explore GitHub's interface. Click on the files, overviews, statistics, and various commits. See what GitHub offers in terms of information about your project—you'll be using it a lot in your future career. If you like, feel free to also explore some of the GUI tools for Git. A comprehensive list is available at the following URL: https://git-scm.com/downloads/guis.

Useful Resources

To learn more about Git, see SitePoint's *Jump Start Git*[9], or Apress's *Pro Git*[10]. Both are newbie-friendly.

If you don't feel like taking the time to read an entire guide, there are helpful illustrated guides at GitHub[11] that cover both Git and GitHub in a very approachable manner. Even though we basically covered both in our usage example before, I recommend going through at least the "Hello World" and "Getting Your Project on GitHub" guides before proceeding with this book. Consider it homework.

Summary

In this chapter, we looked at version control systems and explained how they work and why they exist. We used an example project to briefly demonstrate what they can do, and suggested some additional learning materials.

In the next chapter, we'll talk about hosting, explaining where to find a server, what to use and what to avoid, how to deploy code to a live server, and more.

---

[9] https://www.sitepoint.com/premium/books/jump-start-git
[10] http://git-scm.com/book/en/v2
[11] https://guides.github.com

Deployment and Hosting

Now that version control is out of the way, it's time to look into deployment and hosting.

Deployment, as you may have learned from previous chapters, refers to the act of putting your locally developed application online for people to use. A deployed application doesn't necessarily mean a publicly available one—it can be an intranet application that is internal to a company, for example; it means it can be used by its target audience.

An application, however, cannot be deployed without being **hosted**; there needs to be a server computer that is its home. In this chapter, we'll talk about both terms in more detail and list some approaches to each. We'll also cover the pros and cons of common approaches and define some terms you'll be hearing a lot throughout your web development career.

Even if you're familiar with aspects of deployment and hosting, it's recommended you read this chapter as it contains up-to-date information on what to avoid and what to select.

Hosting

We'll explain hosting first, as it's important to know how to pick a home before you move into one.

The three main types of hosting you'll repeatedly encounter are: shared hosting, cloud hosting, and (virtual) private hosting. I'll explain the parenthesized "virtual" further on.

Shared Hosting

When hosting companies have a single server (which can consist of either a single machine or several acting as one), they make a separate folder and user account for each customer on this server; this is known as **shared hosting**. Each customer is allotted a part of the server's processing power, a fraction of its total RAM, and a chunk of the hard drive space. This **shard** of resources can then be used as a home for your deployed application. A company might have several such servers set up for when one runs out of space to accommodate new users. This sounds great in theory, but in practice it has many problems.

Shared Hosting is Bad

For lack of better (that is, cheaper and/or simpler) options, shared hosting was the only viable approach for many people for a long, long time. This kind of widespread use lead to its dominance of the hosting market, and it remains popular purely because of this initial inertia.

Shared hosting is bad for several reasons:

- *Security risk*: many popular content management systems such as WordPress, Drupal, Joomla, and others ask the user to enable write-all access mode on certain folders so that they may place their files in there. In doing this, many users unwittingly allow access to their website's files by mistake while sharing a hard drive with other customers. This so-called "777 problem" (where 777 is Linux code for "allow everyone to do everything on this file or in this folder") is a tremendous security risk. What's more, when using content management systems on shared hosts, you're at risk of outdated versions. One site's laziness and unwillingness to update another instance of the installed CMS on the same server can lead to *your* site being hacked, as it can become a gateway through which attackers gain access to the entire server!

▨ *Traffic overload*: You rely on other people's competence and traffic. If a site on a given server has badly written code that uses too many CPU cycles or eats up a lot of RAM, other applications on the same server may suffer because of it; since all applications are sharing the same hardware—which is quite limited in shared hosting environments—a user's excessive needs may be detrimental to your own application. The same goes for well-written code with lots of traffic: if another site receives too much traffic, the server might get overloaded and shut down, taking your site down with it.

▨ *Limits*: a lot of shared hosting companies promise unlimited bandwidth and resources, but this is almost never true[1]. There is no such thing as "unlimited" anything: as soon as your site manages to breach an internally agreed-upon limit (be it regular CPU use, hard drive space, or bandwidth), you'll be sure to discover just what unlimited really means. Check out the following piece from WhoIsHostingThis.com that points out the pitfalls of shared hosting, and provides a cautionary tale about getting disconnected due to using up too many resources on an unlimited plan.[2]

▨ *Reputation*: when you're on the same server as other customers, you all share an IP address. Any illicit activity done by others on the same server can reflect badly on you as well. Imagine a customer sending millions of spam emails from a shared hosting server that you use. These emails are then picked up by popular spam-hunting engines and the IP address is flagged as one that often spams people. Suddenly, all emails that your own application sends out are also flagged as spam in people's inboxes, purely because the IP address is the same as that of the original spammer.

These are just some of the main issues around shared hosting. But there's one that's arguably more important than all the others mentioned: shared hosting holds you back.

---

[1] http://myboringchannel.com/the-truth-about-web-hosting/
[2] http://www.whoishostingthis.com/blog/2010/08/09/the-cautionary-tale-of-the-frogpants-network-and-unlimited-hosting/

Shared Hosting Holds You Back

When using shared hosting, you're typically given a simplified user interface such as cPanel, the one shown in Figure 6.1, through which to configure your site. There is, however, no actual server access to fine-tune aspects of your site, install custom extensions, upgrade your app the way you upgrade your local development server, and so on. Essentially, you're locked into what the hosting company has installed and there's no way to change it because it would affect hundreds—maybe thousands—of other users.

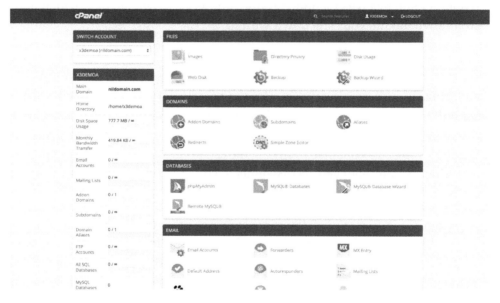

Figure 6.1. cPanel is a common shared-hosting control panel

This might seem ideal for entry-level users, but it provides too much abstraction. In other words, it places a user too far from the nitty-gritty of custom configuration and server setups—something that is absolutely essential to be familiar with in your web development career.

By sticking with such simple approaches, you do yourself a short-term favor for long-term harm. The time *will* come when you'll have to deploy to a real, non-shared server, or when you'll need to manually update server software.

But there *must* be some use cases where all this simplicity is good, right?

Shared Hosting is Good for Limited Use Cases

There are projects where shared hosting is a godsend. In a career of serious web development, these use cases are rare but still possible:

- *Custom email*: with shared hosts, it's incredibly easy to set up a custom email address. Ever dreamed about having an email address such as `firstname@lastname.com`? Would look cool on a business card. With shared hosting, it's a breeze. You buy a domain (`lastname.com`), go into your shared hosting account's control panel, and set it all up according to the instructions. Most have a step-by-step process, so you should have a personalized email account within 24 hours.

- *Small code samples*: those requiring very few resources are easily hosted on shared hosting servers. Small portfolio scripts and projects are ideal for this purpose; for example, code demos within tutorials you write, sample code from client websites you've built, and so on. Anything not needing to support large amounts of bandwidth should work indefinitely, and live demos instead of words on a resume always looks better!

- *Fire-and forget projects*: Finally, there's the simple sites for really low-maintenance clients such as a neighbor's pet, your grandma, a butcher, or a local store. Maybe you're actively involved with volunteer work and are helping to organize a conference by creating a website for them. Anything that's generally short-lived or updated rarely (also known as a fire-and-forget project) has a comfy home on a shared hosting server. The low resource demands of such projects and their relatively limited traffic ensure their compatibility for a long time to come. For a cost as low as $5 per month (the average price of shared hosting servers these days), you can accommodate multiple clients. What's more, the simplicity of the UI and ease of use ensure that the project can be easily taken over by someone else if you're no longer interested in being involved.

Cloud Hosting

Cloud hosting is where many computers are linked in a symbiosis making them act and appear as one.

In Figure 6.2, the horizontal units in the glass cases are minimized computers: hardware units with all the unnecessary parts stripped out so that they are as power, space, and heat efficient as possible. Networked together, they form one great whole, and there are warehouses upon warehouses of them. Contrary to their name, cloud computer systems are very much grounded. They're merely very large computers formed of many little ones.

Figure 6.2. A large collection of servers

On this apparent single computer, a special kind of software is run that dictates the look and feel of the environment; for example, making it seem like we're dealing with a single Linux server. In some ways it's like shared hosting—but on a much, much greater scale (many more computers).

Cloud hosting usually allows terminal access to the server (enabling you to manually configure some items) but often features GUI elements that are used to generate access codes, install plugins into your cloud-powered applications, and more.

Some popular cloud hosting providers are:

- Google App Engine (https://cloud.google.com/appengine/docs)
- Heroku (https://www.heroku.com/)
- Amazon Web Services (https://aws.amazon.com/)
- OpenShift (https://www.openshift.com/)
- Azure (https://azure.microsoft.com/en-us/)

■ Fortrabbit (http://www.fortrabbit.com/)

... and there are many more.

There are several approaches to cloud hosting, but the one common vector they all share is that you do not depend on other customers' good will and code, unlike with shared hosting. The resources of *the cloud* (aka the network of computers on which your app is operating) are focused on processing your (and other people's) code, while the hard drive storage parts (such as storing images your users upload, for example) are usually saved elsewhere. This has two advantages:

1. The cloud is used exclusively to process code. It is optimized for that one purpose, so your app is always fast (depending on your code's quality, of course).
2. There are no resource limits. In cloud computing, there are so many machines working as one that there are always plenty of resources for your app if needed.

Cloud hosting follows a payment model that charges by the number of units of time your app has been using a server. For example, it might be priced at two cents per unit of time per CPU, and units may be increments of 15 minutes. So if your application used one CPU core for 24 hours, then had a sudden traffic spike and used four cores for 24 more hours, you'd end up paying $1.9 for day one, and around $7.7 for day two, totaling around $10 for two days. Cloud hosting is more expensive if you have lots of traffic, but more reliable than shared hosting as it rarely, if ever, crashes. It can also auto-scale (if you tell it to), which means that if your site suddenly receives a huge traffic boost (maybe it ended up on the news), the cloud-hosting provider can automatically allocate more CPU cores to your app and keep it alive for those extra visitors. This means no lost business, which probably offsets those hosting costs anyway! Besides, if you fear a wave of traffic so powerful it could financially destroy you, most services offer limits you can set; for example, "throw more power at my app as long as it stays under $2,000 per month."

Many cloud hosting services also offer free tiers, meaning you can use them free of charge, no strings attached, for as long as you want—but with limited resources and missing features (no custom domains, for example). If you want to expand, you can very easily upgrade the account your site is already hosted on, and it immediately becomes more powerful (and more expensive).

Cloud hosting is *the* hosting choice these days, particularly for high-profile applications requiring extreme reliability, as downtimes are rare. Cloud hosting is also excellent for one-off projects such as demos and portfolio pieces if you utilize the free tiers many offer—at no cost, you can have permanently available, publicly accessible runnable code live online.

It's not all fun and games, though. Some of the disadvantages of shared hosting are present in cloud hosting, too:

- *Vendor lock-in*: this can happen in cloud hosting, too. Often, the platform you're on will have platform-specific settings you need to learn and tweaks to master. Likewise, versions of installed software also tend to remain unpatched. Since the servers are tweaked to run a specific version of, for example, PHP at incredible speeds, that version is also tweaked to run well in such an environment, making it difficult to update as a new version would require those (often non-trivial) tweaks applied as well.
- *Learning limitations*: while shared hosting holds you back by failing to teach you anything about server management, cloud hosting is limiting by teaching you only a *specific type* of server management—theirs. Moving from Google App Engine to Heroku is no trivial operation, both in code terms and in the learning curve involved in mastering a new tool with its own specific commands and utilities.

Remember—cloud hosting is similar to shared hosting, but on a much grander scale. To use cloud hosting, however, one is typically an advanced user already proficient in some server management. For the case of a newbie starting out, I'd always recommend virtual private servers.

(Virtual) Private Hosting

Also known as dedicated hosting, **private hosting** promises a dedicated machine—be it virtual or real—for your needs (hence why virtual is parenthesized). You can then use this machine for whatever purpose you see fit. If you choose to make it into your own shared hosting provider, you can set up the server to support this and resell the space. You could also buy several machines, and cluster them up to make your own mini cloud. Or just use a single server for a single app—that works, too!

In dedicated hosting, having a physical machine just for yourself is quite expensive, getting into thousands of dollars per month depending on the machine's power. That's why most users opt for VPS (virtual private servers), which are virtual machines, or VMs (not unlike Vagrant machines we talked about in previous chapters) on a single server. Much like in cloud and shared hosting, a single computer (or what appears to be one) contains several smaller ones—**instances** for customers to use. These instances act like real servers, so you gain full access to them via the terminal. You can install and uninstall anything at all, even change the operating system. The VM doesn't care; it's completely isolated from the rest, and you can make it and break it at will.

VPS hosting is the most accessible approach for new users for the following reasons:

- *Price:* modern VPS providers are incredibly cheap. Services such as Vultr[3] and DigitalOcean[4] provide virtual servers—machines more than strong enough for the average web app or two—for as little as five dollars per month. This is cheaper than cloud hosting, but much more powerful than shared hosting. The bandwidth is unlimited, and the only CPU, RAM, and hard drive limits you have are those you agree on upon purchase. All servers can also be upgraded at any time, and with programs such as DigitalOcean's referral system, you can end up never paying for a single month if you refer enough people to the service. In fact, the bonus goes both ways: even the ones coming in via a referral link receive a bonus of (currently) ten dollars just for signing up, giving the referrer a bonus after they've actually made a purchase.

- *Reliability:* VPS is as reliable as you make it. Very rarely does an entire data center of machines go offline for such a hosting provider, as there are a plethora of fail-safes installed to prevent downtime from happening. For the most part, the server's stability depends entirely on how you set it up, which leads to you training yourself in server matters—something of utmost importance. When compared to cloud hosting, reliability of the infrastructure behind the scenes is identical; the only real risk of downtime is the customer misconfiguring their VPS instance.

- *Familiarity:* a VPS will look familiar if you started with Vagrant VMs as described in this book. It will be the same interface, same commands, same procedures. You'll be familiar with most of the aspects you can modify, and able to debug your live server because you have experience on your local one (the local Vagrant VM you're developing on). A VPS is a quick and easy way to development-pro-

---

[3] https://www.vultr.com/
[4] http://digitalocean.com

duction parity, which is not as easy to achieve with cloud hosting, and impossible to achieve with shared hosting.

I *always* recommend VPS hosting to new developers because it's the perfect middle ground between cloud hosting's power and shared hosting's ease of use, once a person is comfortable enough with the terminal.

Others

There are, of course, countless other types of hosting as well—each matching specific use cases.

For example, Nitrous.IO[5], Codenvy[6], Cloud9[7], and Koding[8] are all cloud-based development environments (Cloud IDEs) with built-in hosting. Opening an account with them will give you a web interface in which to edit your code—much like in an IDE such as PhpStorm—and at the same time a place to automatically host and run the code you write. These services can be costly for apps that go any measure beyond basic, but are extremely practical for people on the go—particularly netbook users who lack the computing power to run VMs, but are always online and prefer to travel light.

Feel free to create an account with any of them and test out their sample applications. Nothing can go wrong, and nor is there a need to be code-literate to understand what's going on.

I've summarized my views on the pros and cons of various hosting options below.

	Shared Hosting	**Cloud Hosting**	**(V)PS**	**Cloud IDEs**
Affordability	★★★★★	★★★	(★★★★★) ★	★★★
Reliability	★★★	★★★★★	★★★★	★★★★★
Ease of use	★★★★★	★★	★★★★	★★★★★

---

[5] https://www.nitrous.io/
[6] https://codenvy.com/
[7] https://c9.io/
[8] https://koding.com/

	Shared Hosting	Cloud Hosting	(V)PS	Cloud IDEs
Customizability	★	★	★★★★★	★
Security	★★	★★★★★	★★★	★★★★★
Performance	★	★★★★★	★★★★	★★★
Hardware limits	★	★★★★★	★★★	★★★

Deployment

Deployment is the act of sending a ready application to a live server so that it can be accessed by its target audience. It also includes pushing updates to an application online when a new feature is added or a bug is fixed.

There are two main types of deployment: manual and automatic.

Manual

Manual deployment involves actively recognizing that the application is at a stage when it's usable by the target audience, or at a stage matching one in the project specification—a document outlining the entire project's development process.

Once deemed ready, the developer takes one of several approaches to deploy the application:

- **FTP**: in the ancient days of Web 1.0, File Transfer Protocol (FTP) was a way to transfer files (duh!) from one server to another. Today, this approach is usually only seen in severely outdated systems and servers such as universities and schools, or shared hosting. Uploading files via FTP requires you to have an FTP client installed on your computer such as FileZilla[9] or Cyberduck.[10] You also need the credentials of the server you're uploading to—usually the server name, a username, and a password. If an application is already deployed and an updated one is being deployed on top, the older one is usually overwritten, which opens the doors to a whole throng of possible bugs. In regards to application deployment, there are better approaches and FTP should be avoided.

---

[9] https://filezilla-project.org/
[10] https://cyberduck.io/?l=en

■ **Rsyncing** involves using a tool called rsync to synchronize the contents of two folders. Rsync works via SSH (Secure Shell), which essentially means you can use it through the terminal without having to install any additional programs. Rsyncing is better than FTPing because SSH is more secure than FTP—unless you're using SCP (Secure Copy Protocol) in FTP (however, SCP in FTP is still suboptimal as any number of things can go wrong, such as files going missing or getting accidentally deleted, and there's little to no way to quickly undo these mistakes.)

■ **Pulling from a repository**: this method uses the Git version control system (see Chapter 5) to push the changes live. Two approaches can be taken: a *push* can be made so that the code goes to a remote server. This is done from the development environment—the local server. More commonly, a *pull* can be made. Pulling is done by the live server—the machine on which the code should eventually end up. Pulling code from development machines is usually not possible and generally discouraged, because opening up outside access to your development machine is a security risk. Instead, a push is first made to a central repository such as GitHub, and then the live server pulls from there. This approach is the most common as it offers the safety and sanctity of infinite undo steps courtesy of version control, and removes any overwrites that may happen due to multiple people working on the same codebase and trying to upload at once.

These are far from the only means of manual deployment, but they are the most popular ones. They're somewhat tedious, though, and tend to take up time and resources that are better spent elsewhere. In software development, the general rule is to automate whatever can be automated. Which brings us to ...

Automatic and Semiautomatic Deployment

There are many tools for automatic deployment: Robo,[11] Deployer,[12] Envoyer,[13] Rocketeer,[14] DeployBot,[15] and so on. They rely on certain pointers in the source code to know when a version of the application is ready for deployment, or on manual triggers from developers, and then take care of the rest automatically.

---

[11] http://robo.li/
[12] http://deployer.org/
[13] https://envoyer.io/
[14] https://github.com/rocketeers/rocketeer
[15] http://deploybot.com/

Practical aspects of automatic deployers are outside the scope of this book but, put simply, this is how they work:

1. You work on some code and then make a commit in Git.
2. You add this commit to the master branch, the main branch of your repository. As a general rule, anything committed into the master branch is ready for production, aka deployment.
3. A tool such as Deployer notices this new commit to the master branch, automatically checks the code for common errors, and if everything is well sends it online for you without you having to move a finger.

The application code will be up to date and you've simply continued to code after your last commit without even needing to check. The tool did it all for you.

Fully automatic deployment of this kind can be risky, though. The tests in the application may not be robust enough, enabling some bugs to slip through because the application is unable to find its own errors.

This is where semiautomatic deployment comes into play—automatic, but with a human element. Once a developer ensures the release (the newest version of the app) is fine, they run a simple command such as `dep deploy` and the tool takes over the rest of the process: preparing the server, making pushes and pulls, clearing cache files, and so on. This is the best of both worlds; the machine does the heavy lifting, but the developer tells it when to do it.

So, of all these tools and approaches, what's the best combination to use?

Recommendation

I'd recommend using manual deployment with an intermediary GitHub repository, and using DigitalOcean for hosting, at least for the first few months. In due time, you should definitely move towards automation—especially as more advanced concepts such as database migrations, cache busting, and file permissions come into play—but for now, this approach will benefit a newbie the most.

GitHub accounts are free, so you can open one at any time and create an arbitrary number of repositories. DigitalOcean is free for the first two months with my referral link,[16] and only five dollars per month subsequently.

Apart from being wallet-friendly, using these two services in tandem will teach you server maintenance basics, improve your Git and GitHub skills, and make you proficient in the most commonly used deployment and hosting services today.

By the end of this book, we'll have used this GitHub and DigitalOcean flow to deploy a simple application.

Summary

In this chapter, we explained the theory behind deployment and hosting and covered the terms you'll meet most often. We went through the basics of how hosting services work, and learned the best approach to take at this stage of your web development career.

In subsequent chapters we'll be putting this theory into practice by using the tools we mentioned to deploy a sample application; however, there's one more critical piece of the puzzle we need to cover first: Composer, the PHP package manager. Stay tuned, we're about to get our hands dirty again.

---

[16] http://bit.ly/do-ref

Composer

This chapter deals exclusively with Composer, the PHP package manager. If you're familiar with the tool, feel free to move onto the next chapter.

Spaghetti Western

Let's talk about what led to the development of Composer in the first place.

Back when PHP was first created, a "web application" consisted of individual files of PHP code which, when used in the right order, solved many of what was then modern web development problems (submitting forms, writing to the database, and so on). If you had a file called **file-a.php** with a specific bit of logic and **file-b.php** with more logic, and you wanted to use them both, you would include them in yet another file, **file-c.php**.

For example, say **file-a.php** has the code:

```php
<?php

$word1 = "Hello";
?>
```

and **file-b.php** has the code:

```php
<?php

$word2 = "World";
?>
```

You could use them in **file-c.php** like so:

```php
<?php

include 'file-a.php';
include 'file-b.php';

echo "I am now using file-a and file-b, yay! {$word1} {$word2}!";
?>
```

This would output:

```
I am now using file-a and file-b, yay! Hello World!
```

With more files, the include lists grew larger and larger. It follows then that PHP applications were mile-long invocations of these helper scripts, one after the other. We call this code **spaghetti code** because it's a mess—one line intertwined with the next, no structure or order, a bit of logic calling another bit of logic that's defined in an arbitrary external location. Spaghetti code is very hostile to other developers (or even the original developer a couple of months later!).

Figure 7.1. Spaghetti mess

With the advent of object-oriented PHP in version 5, we gained the ability to write blocks of code called **classes**. A class grouped together logic that belonged in a specific context. Specifically, in the realm of the Web, a User class could have the methods (aka internal functions, abilities) login and logout.

In an application, using this class would allow a developer to implement login and log-out functionality. Classes could talk to other classes by **including** them just like the files above (for example, a User class could *include* a Database class in order to use it to check if the database contains the matching username and password combination), but has the added advantage of being transparent about their context. After all, it was very easy to find out what a certain class was intended to do by just looking inside its file, or even at its name alone.

Different classes with related contexts are called a **package** (also known as a **library**). In the same package, one class could be dedicated to handling user logins and logouts, another to sending "reset password" emails, yet another to checking the role of a user (admin, guest), and so on. The whole package could then be called `Authentication`.

But as packages and classes proliferated, the problem of **collisions** appeared. If I had a class `User` and borrowed, for example, Jim's `User` class, trying to use them at the same time to get the best of both worlds would cause an error in PHP (maybe his `User` class also supported profile picture uploads, which mine lacked). Two classes cannot have the same name because PHP has no idea which of the two classes to use! In PHP version 5.3, this problem was solved with namespaces.

Namespaces and Ye Olde Package Management

A common feature in some other languages, **namespaces** found their way into PHP with version 5.3. They sound intimidating, but in reality they're literally just prefixes in front of PHP class names.

The aforementioned `User` class by our buddy Jim would thus be called `Jim\User` (the backslash \ is special notation used to separate fragments of namespaces; this allows namespaces to be nested into an arbitrary number of levels), while ours could be called `SitePoint\Authentication\User`. While their final "name" is the same (`User`), their fully qualified names are different, and PHP is happy to let us use both at the same time.

But still, using several packages and classes means we have to include them all, just like the previous example above—one file "calling" the others by filename, making sure they're summoned for use. There are some ways around this, of course—special functions called "autoloaders" were developed that looked for classes in locations based on their names (for example, `Jim\User` could be in `classes\Jim\User.php`); however, it is still tedious to not only find other people's classes, but also effectively include them and make them conform to the autoloader function in use.

To solve this problem, we use a tool called Composer.

What is Composer?

Composer[1] is a package manager for PHP. We already defined a *package* as a collection of classes. So what's a package manager, then?

A **package manager** is a tool that removes the human element from the process of finding and installing packages or programs into an environment. If you're using OS X, for example, there is a package manager for the OS called Homebrew. Rather than scour the Web in search of an application such as MPlayer, a media player, one can use the terminal to run the command:

```
brew install mplayer
```

Like magic, the application will be installed and instantly available. On Linux operating systems, there are several package managers. A popular one is Aptitude and is used in a similar fashion:

```
sudo apt-get install chrome
```

This command installs the latest Chrome browser, just like that.

Package managers make sure *packages* (an application *is* a package—it's a set of files working together towards a singular purpose, be it media playback, web browsing, or something else entirely) are installed cleanly, quickly, and safely.

Similarly, in the context of programming languages (such as PHP), a package manager is used to retrieve, install, update, and uninstall packages. While the grunt work of setting up autoloading for classes without Composer is easy enough, Composer removes the process completely. It automates the manual process of finding a package online, downloading it, unzipping, putting it into your project's folder, including it, configuring it, and so on.

Composer ties into Packagist,[2] the *de facto* online directory of packages from PHP users. Let's explain what happens when you install a package with Composer.

---

[1] http://getcomposer.org

[2] http://packagist.org

Installing packages with Composer is as easy as calling Composer's `require` command while inside the folder of your application:

```
composer require nesbot/carbon
```

At this point Composer will, in order:

1. Look at the argument after `require` and determine that it is a valid package name. Note that package names use the normal forward slash (/).
2. Look at its configuration (a special file called **composer.json**) for information on where to find `nesbot/carbon`. No information is found, so it will move to the next step.
3. Go to Packagist and look up the entry for `nesbot/carbon`. If it's there, it then moves to the next step.
4. Read the configuration of that package to find out if the package itself has any **dependencies** (which are other packages it needs to do what it does). It then starts the process over for each of them before finishing `nesbot/carbon`.
5. After all dependencies have been installed, it downloads `nesbot/carbon`, updates an autoload file (located in the main project's folder, under **vendor/autoload.php** by default), and makes sure the newly installed package is usable in your application.

To use this package, ensure that the aforementioned **autoload.php** file is included in your app. This only needs to be done once, regardless of how many packages you install. They're all autoloaded with this one file:

```php
<?php

include 'vendor/autoload.php';
```

This might seem a bit abstract, so let's see it in action.

Usage Example

PHP has a built-in class called `DateTime` (documented at http://php.net/manual/en/class.datetime.php), which can be used to do time-related calculations and operations. The class is somewhat unintuitive, however.

The `nesbot/carbon` package has a single class with the ability to manipulate time. Well, not manipulate time per se—PHP isn't *that* powerful (yet!)—but to manipulate `DateTime` values.

Carbon was developed as an upgrade of `DateTime`, and lets you use very human expressions to obtain the values you need. Let's try and use this handy package! As per the Carbon instructions,[3] we could just download, unzip, and manually include it in our project with `include 'Carbon.php'`; however, it really is recommended that you use Composer every chance you can.

Bootstrapping

We start off by booting up a new virtual machine, as per Chapter 4. The following five commands executed from the host computer's terminal do everything for us:

```
git clone https://github.com/swader/homestead_improved hi_carbontest
cd hi_carbontest;
bin/folderfix.sh
vagrant up
vagrant ssh
```

The last command enters the VM, so you're inside it, as if connected to a server. Then, execute:

```
cd Code
touch index.php
```

The `touch` command creates an empty file with the given name.

Open this **index.php** file with your text editor or IDE of choice, either in the terminal with `vim index.php` or on your host machine by going into the folder and double clicking on it. Then give it the content:

```
<?php

echo "Hello World";
```

Save and exit the file, then in the terminal inside the VM run:

---

[3] https://github.com/briannesbitt/Carbon

```
php index.php
```

You should see "Hello World" appear onscreen.

 Command Line Interface Mode

In this instance, we are executing PHP on the command line for the sake of simplicity. In other words, we're not using the browser to see the output. Rather, we're having PHP print its output on the screen of the terminal. This is also called **CLI mode**, which is short for "Command Line Interface."

Installing Carbon

Composer usually has to be manually installed onto fresh servers, but our Homestead Improved VM comes with Composer pre-installed and accessible from any location, so all we need to do is execute:

```
composer require nesbot/carbon
```

As soon as the procedure is done, reopen the **index.php** file from earlier, and add a new line after <?php so that it now looks like this:

```
<?php

include 'vendor/autoload.php';

echo "Hello World";
```

Including the **vendor/autoload.php** file ensures that the classes we install with Composer are automatically loaded into our application, without the need for manually specifying include or require statements to combine them all into one app.

Testing

Now that Carbon is installed and autoloaded into our application, we can give it a try.

In **index.php**, instead of the Hello World line, add the following code so that the file now looks like this:

```
<?php

include 'vendor/autoload.php';

echo Carbon\Carbon::now();
echo "\n";
```

The last line prints out a blank line, so the output looks prettier.

Then, in the terminal, run `php index.php`. You should see a message not unlike Figure 7.2.

Figure 7.2. Example output

It works! Let's find out what day of the week it will be this time in five years by adding the line:

```
echo Carbon\Carbon::now()->addYears(5)->dayOfWeek;
```

You should see output similar to Figure 7.3.

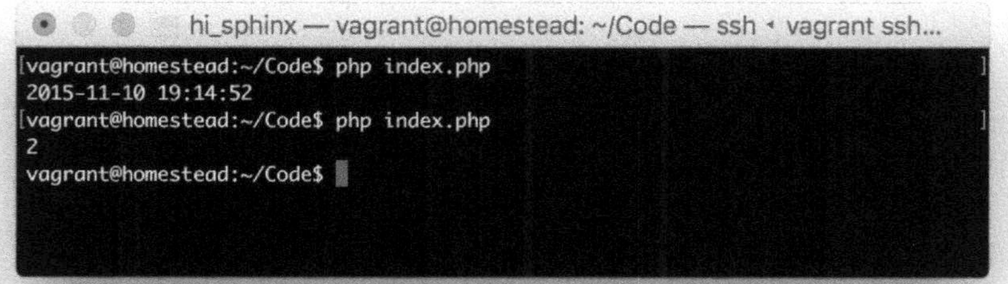

Figure 7.3. Example output 2

This first creates a new "current time" with now(), adds five years to it, and then grabs the day of week out of that value. Days start on Sunday (0), so Wednesday is 3, Friday is 5, and so on. In the example output, we got back Tuesday.

We've successfully installed and used the Carbon package in just a few lines of code.

Cleanup

As we have no need for this VM anymore, nor this Carbon experiment, feel free to delete it with the following commands:

```
exit                   # this exits the virtual machine
vagrant destroy        # this shuts down and deletes the VM
cd ..                  # this goes up one folder
rm -rf hi_carbontest   # this deletes the hi_carbontest folder
```

More Tricks to Try

There are some other commands and features worth mentioning.

Update versus Install and Composer Lock

When a package is installed with Composer, a **composer.json** file is automatically created. Here's the file that was created after we installed Carbon in the earlier example:

```
{
    "require": {
        "nesbot/carbon": "^1.21"
    }
}
```

The format you're seeing here is called JSON,[4] but it's beyond this book's purview. Feel free to explore it on your own. What we can see here is that Composer automatically figured out that 1.21 is the most recent version of Carbon and put that into the file.

Likewise, a **composer.lock** file was created. As it's a bit too large to include in this book, let's look at the relevant segment only:

```
        ⋮
"packages": [
        {
            "name": "nesbot/carbon",
            "version": "1.21.0",
            "source": {
                "type": "git",
                "url": "https://github.com/briannesbitt/Carbon.git",
                "reference": "7b08ec6f75791e130012f206e3f7b0e76e18
➥e3d7"
            },
            "dist": {
                "type": "zip",
                "url": "https://api.github.com/repos/briannesbitt/
➥Carbon/zipball/7b08ec6f75791e130012f206e3f7b0e76e18e3d7",
                "reference": "7b08ec6f75791e130012f206e3f7b0e76e18
➥e3d7",
                "shasum": ""
            },

        ⋮
```

It seems to have the same requirements listed, but in a much more verbose way. What gives?

---

[4] http://www.json.org/

The **composer.lock** file is used to list all the installed dependencies at a given time. **composer.lock** is then committed (see Chapter 5) into your application's repository along with all source code, and on the live server (when deploying). `composer install` then looks for this file. If the command finds it, it will use the versions listed in this file—**no matter how outdated!** If there is no lock file, it will look for the newest versions of the required packages, generate a completely new **composer.lock** file, and proceed as usual.

Why is this important?

Imagine using PackageX v1.2 in your local development environment, testing your application, and after ensuring it all works, deploying it to a live server. Yet in the time between your checks and the app being deployed, PackageX was updated to v1.3, which differs from v1.2 enough to no longer share some functionality. Maybe a method was renamed? Letting Composer determine the newest version on its own would install the latest version and make your app use a non-existent method, thus crashing the application. Disaster! That's why **composer.lock** is there—to ensure the version that was used in development is what's installed.

So, how do we then update the package to 1.3 if we *actually want to*? We use the `composer update` command.

`composer update` looks at all the installed packages, regardless of the presence of a **composer.lock** file, updates both **composer.json** and **composer.lock** with the newest versions, and installs them. Typically, `composer update` is run only in development (not production); when you're certain everything works with the latest version, the newly generated **composer.lock** is deployed with the app as usual, and `composer install` is run in production, again ensuring only the versions *locked* by **composer.lock** are installed.

`require-dev` and `global`

During development, it's common to write unit tests for your code. A final version of your application/package, however, can omit those tests. Tests are for development, to make sure the code works. Including them in final versions of your work bloats the file size without any benefit to end users (though it is good for developers who want to contribute to your code).

For this purpose, a `--dev` option exists when calling `composer require`. For example, if I'm using a package called PHPUnit to write my unit tests, I would install it like so:

```
composer require phpunit/phpunit --dev
```

This places it in a special `require-dev` block in **composer.json**, rather than `require`, and ensures it stays out of the end user's way when a package is installed with the `--update-no-dev` flag. For example, we developed `SitePoint\Authorization\User` with PHPUnit for tests, but Jim just wants to use the package only—no need for tests. He installs it with:

```
composer require sitepoint/auth-user --update-no-dev
```

PHPUnit, however, is a tool which is useful across many projects, but installing it for each one is wasteful, as it's quite large. That's where `global` comes in. The `global` option of the `composer require` command will make sure it's installed as a *global package*, instantly becoming available across the entire operating system we're working on:

```
composer global require phpunit/phpunit --dev
```

Is that all there is?

Of course not! Composer has a multitude of commands. All the above and much more is what makes Composer an essential tool in a PHP developer's daily routine. From removing the mental overhead of tracking used packages and classes, to smooth updates and flawless cooperation with other Composer users, this package manager continues to take the PHP ecosystem by storm.

There's also the very useful `scripts` block, which lets a package author execute arbitrary scripts in the various stages of a command's execution (that is, before installing or after updating), the `composer remove` command for removing packages you no longer need, and so on.

However, this is not a Composer book, so we'll avoid going into the full details here. Instead, I suggest you have a look at the tutorials at the end of this chapter. They include not only a top-down introduction into Composer that's a bit more advanced than what you went through here, but list tips, tricks, and shortcuts to use with it, maximizing the tool's potential.

At this point in your programming career you'll only be using it occasionally, and what you learned here will be enough; once you progress further, you should find these tutorials invaluable.

For Those Who Want More

If you'd like to explore the concepts of modern PHP applications in depth, I cannot recommend Paul M. Jones' book enough. *Modernizing Legacy Applications in PHP*[5] is a complete hands-on guide to turning spaghetti code into maintainable object-oriented professional code. While it probably would be unwise to dive into that book without first going through a beginner-friendly PHP coding book such as *PHP and MySQL: Novice to Ninja*,[6] I wholeheartedly recommend you put it on your to-read list for later.

Additionally, some useful tutorials on SitePoint related to the material presented in this chapter can be found at the following links:

- Namespaces introduction: http://www.sitepoint.com/php-53-namespaces-basics/
- Composer introduction:
  http://www.sitepoint.com/php-dependency-management-with-composer/
- Composer cheat sheet: http://www.sitepoint.com/composer-cheatsheet/
- Mastering Composer—tips and tricks:
  http://www.sitepoint.com/mastering-composer-tips-tricks/

---

[5] https://leanpub.com/mlaphp
[6] https://www.sitepoint.com/premium/books/phpmysql5

Chapter 6

Learn by Example: A Web App from Scratch

It's time to put everything we've learned so far to use—and then some! In this chapter, we'll build a simple database-powered PHP application and deploy it online. We'll explore different approaches to each aspect while keeping it all as newbie-friendly as possible.

Some aspects, such as databases and frameworks, are yet to be covered in the book, so they'll be briefly introduced in this chapter. As usual, the end of the chapter will list links that are useful for further expanding one's knowledge of modern web app development practices.

This chapter is the whole point of the book—demonstration of an app-building process—so skipping it is not an option.

Note that the content you'll encounter throughout this chapter is likely to make you feel overwhelmed—even frustrated if you're entirely unfamiliar with PHP code. That's fine. In programming it's called the hump, and you just have to power through it. You're just encountering it a little earlier than most newbies, but avoid letting it frighten you. If you struggle to understand the code, go through it again and try to comprehend what it does based on the explanations under the code snippets, but don't force it. Take it for granted for now, and return when it becomes a little clearer. No one understood everything on the first go. Besides, the point of this chapter is to demonstrate the initialization of a development environment and the deployment of an app. Everything learned in between is what I'd call *collateral profit*.

What will we be building?

We'll craft a guestbook application. If you're a young millennial, you might not know what a guestbook application is. A guestbook application was, in the ancient times of the simpler Web, a way to leave feedback on a site; it applied to the site in general, rather than being comments on a particular article or post, like it is today.

Guestbooks are rarely encountered these days, but the principles used to build a guestbook app apply to building comment systems for per-post usage, hand-crafted forums, and more.

Our app (seen in Figure 8.1) will have the following features:

■ a common HTML input form for comments
■ display previously entered comments above the input form

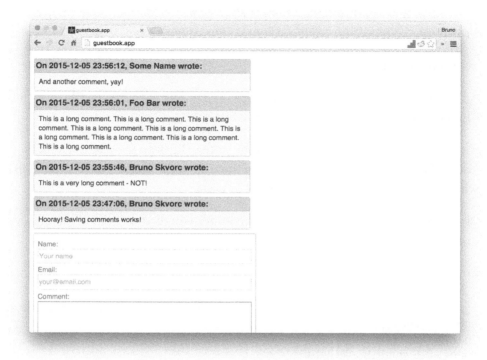

Figure 8.1. The complete app

The guestbook app will be accessible in our development environment (see Chapter 2) via http://guestbook.app.

Note that .app is a valid TLD (see Chapter 1 for an explanation of top-level domains), so be careful with adding new `etc/hosts` entries under it; you might block access to *real* `.app` websites if they start appearing. To be completely safe, use any of the following suffixes instead: .test, .example, .localhost and .invalid.

Setting Up the Environment

Let's set up our environment (this process is described in detail in Chapter 4). Before proceeding, please make sure you have installed the following:

- Vagrant, from https://www.vagrantup.com/
- VirtualBox, from https://www.virtualbox.org/
- Git, from http://git-scm.com/downloads

If you followed along through all the previous chapters, particularly Chapter 4, you're all set.

To set up the environment:

1. Add the line `192.168.10.10 guestbook.app` to our `/etc/hosts` file. See the Chapter 3 for details on how and why to do this.

2. If your operating system is Windows, open the Git Bash program, which is available after installing Git tools from the link at the start of the section. Otherwise, open the Terminal app on Linux or OS X.

3. Change directory (by typing `cd`) into the folder where you'd like to develop your project. A good place is your user's home folder: `cd ~`.

4. Enter the following commands:

```
git clone https://github.com/swader/homestead_improved hi_guestapp
cd hi_guestapp
bin/folderfix.sh
mkdir -p guestbook/public
mkdir guestbook/storage
touch guestbook/public/index.php
```

The last three commands create the folders our application will need, and an empty `index.php` file into which we'll later put some PHP code.

5. Open the file **Homestead.yaml** in that folder and add a new `sites` pairing so that the final version looks like:

```
sites:
    - map: homestead.app
      to: /home/vagrant/Code/Project/public
    - map: guestbook.app
      to: /home/vagrant/Code/guestbook/public
```

6. After saving the file, in the terminal run:

```
vagrant up; vagrant ssh
```

Notice how we're using ; between commands? This chains them so that they are executed one after the other without us having to wait for one's output to proceed with the other.

Finally, we need to open the folder guestbook in our code editor of choice. Figure 8.2 shows it in PhpStorm.[1]

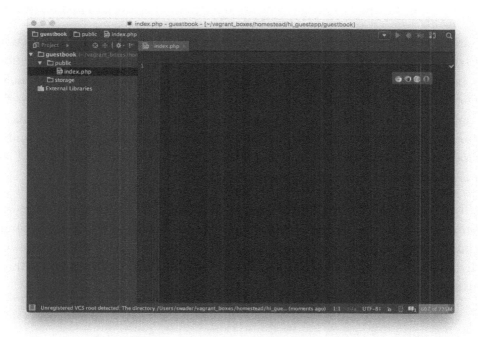

Figure 8.2. Our project open in PhpStorm

It's completely empty right now, but that's about to change.

Bootstrapping the App

Bootstrapping means establishing a setup for future work. In the context of web app development, it means laying the foundation for development and getting the common preparatory steps out of the way.

Before we do this, there are some terms we need to cover.

---

[1] https://www.jetbrains.com/phpstorm/

Testing

In programming, there is a concept known as **testing**. While testing is outside the scope of this book (see the end of the chapter for links to further reading), I'll explain it briefly.

Whenever you make a change in one of your apps, you usually refresh the app in the browser to ensure the changes have been applied. This is called **manual testing**.

There are tools that automate this process. By writing a specific set of instructions (*tests*), your application can *test itself* after every change. Writing these instructions can be complicated and time-consuming, but as an application grows, the time invested in writing tests pays off several times over. No longer does one need to, for example, click every link of a web page to make sure it works; the tests do this automatically, and outside of the traditional browser (with programs that simulate a browser behind the scenes). This makes them much faster than humans and less error-prone (due to removing the human element).

We'll skip automatic testing in this chapter, as it would be too complex to explain (again, see the links at the end of the chapter for resources on testing). In general, no application—regardless of complexity—should be without tests if its purpose is to live longer than a few days or a few visitors (our demo app does not have these constraints).

Our first manual test will be making sure we receive a blank page if we go to the http://guestbook.app URL in the browser, as shown in Figure 8.3.

Figure 8.3. No news is good news

No errors is a good sign. It means that our empty PHP file was reached, and gave the browser its content. In this case, the content is literally *nothing*.

Frameworks versus Packages

Chapter 7 mentioned packages: they are sets of reusable code. There is, however, another level beyond packages: PHP frameworks.

A **framework** is a predefined set of packages designed to quickly bootstrap an application; the traditional process of setting up database connections, login systems, and more are dealt with by having it all pre-built. This means most frameworks are either very opinionated (that is, they enforce their particular way of doing things, such as Laravel[2]) or incredibly extensible and hyper-configurable, but over-engineered (thousands of lines of code handling what could be done in a dozen lines, all for the sake of remaining fully configurable, such as Symfony[3]).

These days, frameworks are often the default starting point for a project. They can be a quick way to skip coding elements that are minor to your project. Some developers shy away from using frameworks because they see them either as too

---

[2] http://laravel.com
[3] http://symfony.com

complex or too restrictive. Still, when contracts are at stake, being able to focus on programming the business logic in a matter of hours rather than days can make or break a job.

In our case, while a framework would get *some* hurdles out of the way, it would introduce *more*. Frameworks are complex beasts consisting of hundreds of classes, and we're yet to even touch on object-oriented programming or design patterns—broad disciplines essential to taming a framework (see the links in the section called "For Those Who Want More"). Therefore, we'll be doing it old-school and pulling in just the packages we need, as we need them, with Composer, which we saw in Chapter 7.

To begin bootstrapping our app, we'll first execute:

```
cd ~/Code/guestbook
composer init
```

This command is generally used for bootstrapping new packages (as in when we intend to develop a reusable package and host it on Packagist—discussed in Chapter 7). It is, however, useful for bootstrapping a new app as well, as it helps the developer define metadata about the project. Once executed, Composer will ask for some information, which should be answered like so:

```
vagrant@homestead:~/Code/guestbook$ composer init


  Welcome to the Composer config generator



This command will guide you through creating your composer.json
➥ config.

Package name (<vendor>/<name>) [root/guestbook]: sitepoint/guestbook
Description []: A guestbook app
Author []: Your Name Here <your@email.here>
Minimum Stability []:
Package Type []: project
License []: MIT

Define your dependencies.
```

```
Would you like to define your dependencies (require) interactively
➥ [yes]? no
Would you like to define your dev dependencies (require-dev)
➥ interactively [yes]? no
```

Minimum stability allows the developer to lower the safety barrier for the stability of packages. For example, a package we want to use may be without a stable version; it might be in beta mode. To be able to install it, we'd have to set `beta` under that option. In this case, we're just hitting **Enter** to leave it at the default.

Package type tells Composer that this is a project rather than a reusable package. This has little to no effect on our app per se. *License* is rather well-explained on the GitHub blog,[4] and you can find out about the rest of the available options in `composer.json` (which the command `composer init` generated) in Composer's documentation.[5]

The final two questions ask us to define which packages we'll need. We don't know yet, so we'll skip them.

Finally, we generate the autoload file:

```
composer install
```

As there are no dependencies defined in either the `require` or the `require-dev` block of **composer.json**, there is nothing to install; the command merely generates an autoload file that will automatically load classes we'll install later. Let's use that file. Give **public/index.php** this content:

```php
<?php

require_once '../vendor/autoload.php';

echo "Hello World";
```

Time for another manual test. Revisiting http://guestbook.app in the browser should produce the message "Hello World" as shown in Figure 8.4. If it does, the PHP code

---

[4] https://github.com/blog/1530-choosing-an-open-source-license
[5] https://getcomposer.org/doc/04-schema.md

was successfully executed past the `require_once` point, indicating that our `autoload` file was loaded without problems.

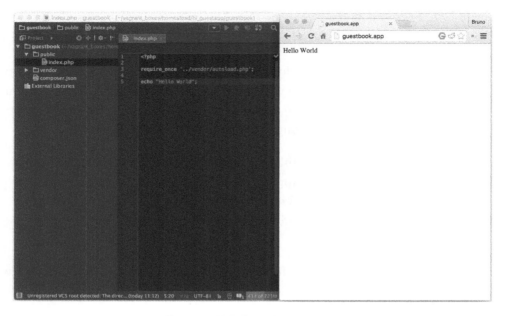

Figure 8.4. "Hello World" loads with ease

`require_once` (see http://php.net/manual/en/function.require-once.php) is a statement telling PHP to "Take the contents of this file and put them into the current one. Crash if you cannot find it!" The `require` part makes sure of this. There are other versions of this statement, all explained on the manual's page.

Developing the App

At last, the fun part! Or is it?

Var Dumper

We'll begin by pulling in the `var-dumper` package, a tool from the Symfony framework (see the section called "Frameworks versus Packages").

Like many other frameworks, Symfony is a collection of packages for solving common web application development problems. When used as a set, they form a solid (albeit complex) starting point for highly customizable web applications. These various

Symfony components are also designed to be used standalone, so if users adopt a custom approach or different framework, they can benefit from Symfony packages.

var-dumper is one such component. PHP has a built-in function called var_dump that outputs the contents of a variable onscreen. The var_dumper component provides a dump function that does the same, but in a more readable manner and with collapser/expander buttons. We'll demonstrate this shortly; for now, let's install it:

```
composer require symfony/var-dumper --dev
```

The --dev option tells Composer to place it in the require-dev block of composer.json. This is because *debugging helpers* of this kind are typically used in development, rather than production. For packages that are required in production, we simply omit the --dev flag and they'll end up in the require block, not require-dev. The rule of thumb is: if a package is meant to be used only during the development phase of an app or another package, put it in require-dev. Otherwise, we can put it in require (by omitting the --dev option). Then, when we deploy our app to production, we'll be able to tell Composer to install with composer install --no-dev, making the installation process much faster.

As we've mentioned, PHP has a built-in "variable dumper"—the function var_dump[6]. Let's try it out on a PHP array. If you're unsure what an **array** is, imagine a box that can contain a variety of items. In **index.php**, add the following:

```
$array = [1, "apple", 2, "foo", "bar"];

var_dump($array);
```

The square brackets in the code are the edges of our hypothetical box—everything between them is placed into the array.

Then, refresh the http://guestbook.app page, and you should see a similar sight to Figure 8.5.

---

[6] http://php.net/manual/en/function.var-dump.php

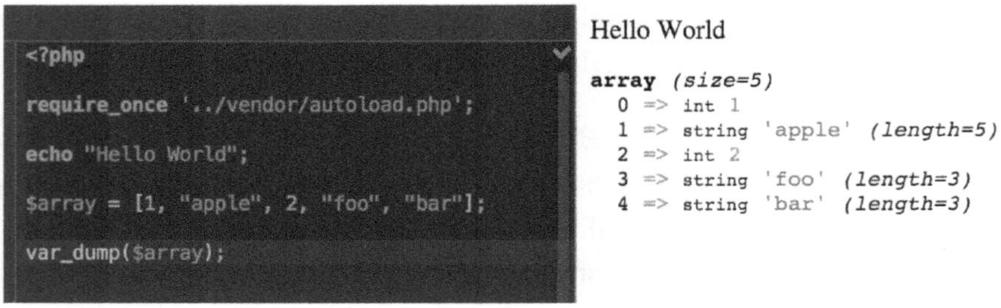

Figure 8.5. Our `var_dump` example

The output is on the right, under "Hello World." It's not exactly unreadable—as Homestead Improved comes with Xdebug installed, a PHP add-on that makes these types of output prettier by default—but it could be better. Let's add in a call to `dump`. The result can be seen in Figure 8.6.

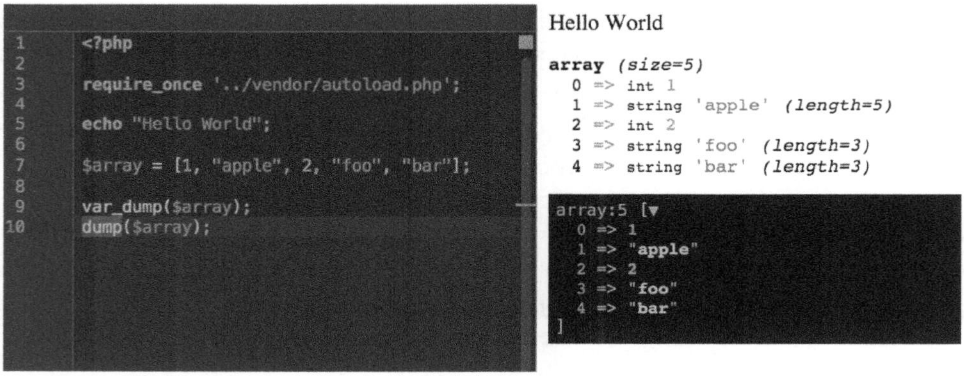

Figure 8.6. An example of dump

Better, no? The collapser/expander button alone is worth it—you can imagine this being tremendously useful when dealing with huge trees of nested arrays (an array can contain an array, which can contain another array, and so on ...).[7]

With `dump` available, we've prepared our development environment for debugging. Should any errors arise, we'll be able to output the information we need in an easily navigable manner.

---

[7] If you're curious, read more about **var-dumper** in this SitePoint post: [http://www.sitepoint.com/var_dump-introducing-symfony-vardumper/]

Database Connection

There are many databases available: MySQL, OracleDB, PostreSQL, MSSQL, SQLite, and so on. The most popular one to use in tandem with PHP is MySQL. Introducing SQL is outside the scope of this book, but it's unnecessary for our purposes anyway—we'll be using a library that *abstracts* database communication for us.

To understand abstraction, imagine a power socket in the EU. It looks like a pig snout, and we call it the Schuko socket, seen in Figure 8.7.

Figure 8.7. Schuko socket, common to the EU

Then imagine a power socket in the US, seen in Figure 8.8. It has two vertical slits and a screaming mouth that is completely incompatible with the EU one.

Figure 8.8. US socket

Every part of the world has its own standard,[8] and if you're a world traveler, carrying a separate power brick for each country you visit would quickly take you past the airline's baggage weight limit (and your budget). Luckily there are items such as socket adapters.

---

[8] http://www.worldstandards.eu/electricity/plugs-and-sockets/

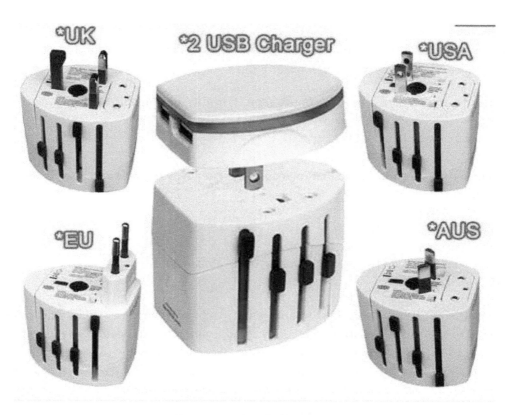

Figure 8.9. A universal socket adapter

One beast such as the one in Figure 8.9 handles most of the world's power sockets. Is it heavier than just carrying one laptop power brick and hoping your destination supports the required socket? Yes, but for a few additional grams, you have all the convenience of ten power bricks with a fraction of the weight. The adapter is an *abstract for a power-providing service.*

The same happens with abstraction in software. We could learn how to communicate with PostreSQL, SQLite, MySQL, MSSQL, and others, sure. It would take a while, but it's possible—just like lugging around ten power bricks. Or we could rely on **abstraction**—letting the authors of the package we put between the database and us do the heavy lifting while we focus on *usage.*

One such database abstraction layer is the very lightweight Medoo package.[9] At only 20KB in file size added to our project, we have the power to communicate with several database engines in exactly the same way.

We'll demonstrate this in an example soon. For now, let's install Medoo:

```
composer require catfan/medoo
```

Change the **index.php** file so that instead of the $array, var_dump and dump lines we added before we now have:

```
$database = new medoo([
    'database_type' => 'sqlite',
    'database_file' => '../storage/database.db'
]);
```

The variable $database is there to hold a new instance of the Medoo class. The class needs a type and a filepath as the constructor arguments—the values required for a class to build its instance properly—so we pass them along in an array. (Notice the square brackets—just like in the array example earlier). The arrows between the left and right column indicate assignment between keys and values—just as in algebra x = 3, so too database_type = sqlite. For links on crash courses in object-oriented programming, please see the end of chapter.

I understand this may feel a bit frustrating if you struggle to fully comprehend the code here and what follows. However, rest assured that understanding the code itself is not all that important; the main aim of this book is to see an example app being started and deployed the right way.

Refresh the browser and if there are no errors, we're good, as seen in Figure 8.10.

---

[9] http://www.sitepoint.com/getting-started-medoo-examples-use/

Figure 8.10. Our database now exists

Additionally, notice how in the storage subfolder of the project a new file appeared: **database.db**. This is because we're using SQLite in this example (there's a good introduction to SQLite on SitePoint[10]), which creates a database file if it doesn't exist.

We could just as easily have put `mysql` or `postgresql` under `database_type` and used that, as they're both pre-installed on Homestead Improved, but that would require additional configuration and wouldn't be as clear outside of Homestead; those database engines need to be installed, after all.

SQLite, on the other hand, is present on almost all operating systems by default, and can be used out of the box. It's not as fast as MySQL and lacks some advanced features, but we need neither this speed nor the complexity in our current project.

The `database_file` value tells Medoo where to create the SQLite file to hold all our saved data. We told it to go "*up one folder, and into storage/database.db*" ; hence, the **database.db** file was created. The `$database` variable is now our adapter, plugged into a wall socket—our access to the data storage.

Try dumping it, just to see what it's made of (Figure 8.11).

---

[10] http://www.sitepoint.com/getting-started-sqlite3-basic-commands/

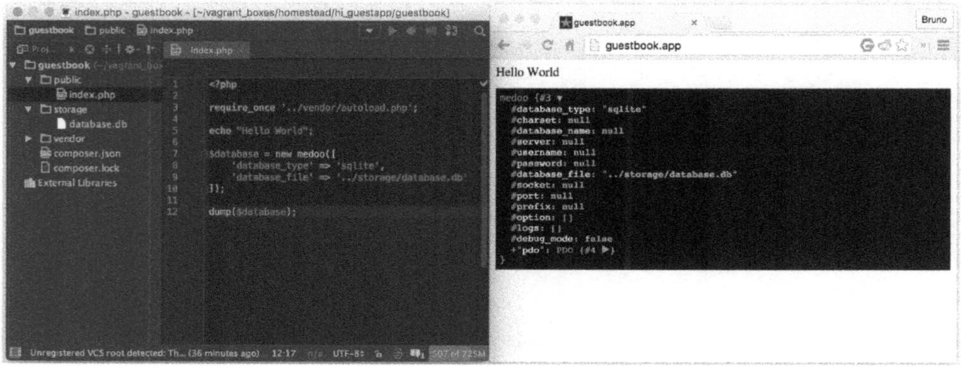

Figure 8.11. Medoo instance

Obviously, there's more beneath the surface, but we needn't concern ourselves with this. The database access works, and that's all that matters right now.

Repo and First Push

At this point, we might as well put our project into version control and upload it to GitHub. Not only will this allow us to share our code with others, but also provide a layer of protection from critical hardware failures.

First, create a repo on GitHub as done in Chapter 5. In my case, that'll be https://github.com/spbooks/phpenv1-example.

Then, in the root folder of our project (inside **guestbook**), run:

```
git init
```

Next, set up a basic **.gitignore** file by downloading the contents of http://bit.ly/spignore or running:

```
curl http://bit.ly/spignore -L > .gitignore
```

If you're curious about the above, curl is a program we use to retrieve the contents of a remote URL, like visiting web pages in the terminal. Next comes the URL the contents of which we want to retrieve, then the -L flag which tells curl to "follow redirects" in case the URL leads to another URL rather than to the end content, and then > **.gitignore** tells it "write the output you get into **.gitignore**".

Then, we need to add a **remote** — we need to let the local repo know where its online home is. In my case, the command is:

```
git remote add origin git@github.com:spbooks/phpenv1-example.git
```

Alter the URL accordingly.

 Adding Vagrant-powered Projects to Version Control

There are two schools of thought regarding committing Vagrant-powered projects to version control. The first one, which matches the general consensus and the official Vagrant docs, is that the Vagrantfile and all its accompanying scripts should be committed to version control alongside a project's source code. If you choose this path, you first remove all traces of version control from the Homestead Improved clone by running `rm -rf .git` inside **hi_guestapp**, and then run `git init` and everything else we describe here from within that folder. Proceed as usual — your whole team now also has your Vagrant setup. This is very handy for teams developing commercial, closed-source apps, because the setup can be dictated for the team.

The second approach, the one I personally favor and that, for the sake of simplicity, we will take in this chapter, is committing only the source code of the project — not its surroundings, such as the Vagrantfile, **Homestead.yaml**, etc. This makes sure it's usable in anyone's development machine, even those who don't use Vagrant or those who use a different box for running test projects. Hence, this approach is best for open source projects where you want to give contributors the freedom to choose their own development environment. This approach is also a bit more lightweight, in terms of filesize. Regardless of the approach you choose, you're not wrong. Pick whatever feels better, or what ever the team you're working with prefers.

On fresh VMs, Git — when used from inside the VM — won't know who's using it. To make yourself known, optionally execute:

```
git config --global user.name "Your Name"
git config --global user.email you@example.com
```

If you're using Git outside the VM to commit the project files (doesn't matter which approach you take, both are just fine), you can skip this step.

To add the files and folders we created so far to the repo and push them online, we execute:

```
git add -A; git commit -m "First commit"; git push -u origin master
```

Figure 8.12. Pushed files

All the files we created thus far (including the database) are now online, as you can see in Figure 8.12. Please note that when developing applications with databases that contain sensitive information (like usernames, passwords, or emails), the database files should **never** be committed into the repository for obvious reasons.

HTML Form

When starting new web projects, there is a useful "boilerplate" we can use with some best practices already built in. While using it is optional, it's preferred purely because when one starts from scratch and implements best practices manually, one tends to eventually end up at the point of this pre-made boilerplate. That boilerplate is called **HTML5 Boilerplate** or H5BP and can be downloaded at https://html5boilerplate.com/.

Unzip its contents into the **public** folder of our project, so that it now looks like Figure 8.13.

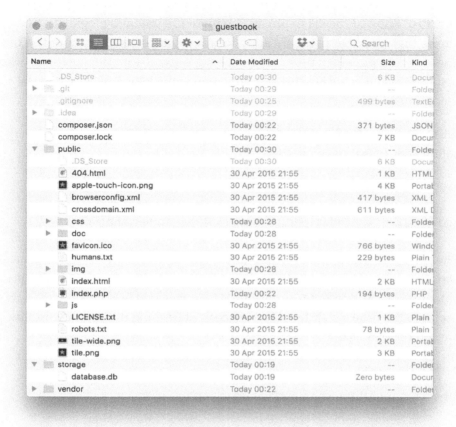

Figure 8.13. New folder structure

As you can see, a whole bunch of new files and folders was added. If you'd like to know more about all these additions, please see H5BP's documentation.

index.php vs index.html

Most servers are configured to first look for an **index.html** file, then for a **index.php** one. Indeed, if you refresh http://guestbook.app now, you'll see the greeting page of H5BP, rather than our output from before.

We could just delete `index.html` and the server would once again serve `index.php`, but then we'd lose the advantages of H5BP. To get our content back, we:

- open `index.php`, and end the file with `?>`. That's the PHP closing tag, and it's how PHP knows it needs to process no more programming logic. It's how it knows that from that point on, all it does is print the stuff it encounters out to the screen. In pure PHP files, the closing tag is usually omitted because it serves no purpose and can cause bugs[11], but when using PHP and HTML in the same file, it's necessary.

- select all contents of `index.php`, and place them in `index.html`, at the very top, before `<doctype>`. Save the file.

- execute the commands:

```
cd public; rm index.php; mv index.html index.php; cd ..
```

The above deletes the old PHP file and turns the HTML file into a PHP one. This way, the server moves directly to `index.php` again, but this time it also prints out all the H5BP content (the various HTML tags that are invisible to us, but useful to the browser and mobile devices). Refreshing the app now produces our old content again.

The HTML Form

Finally, we can build the comment submission form.

In place of `<p>Hello world! This is HTML5 Boilerplate.</p>`, we need to put the following:

```
<form method="post">

    <input type="submit" value="Save">
</form>
```

This is the beginning and end of our form. The `method` attribute on the opening `form` tag means "send a POST request". The default is GET which, when a form is submitted, puts all the values of the various form elements into the URL (e.g. http://guestbook.app?name=bruno&email=bruno.skvorc@sitepoint.com&comment=...) which is not something we want. GET is typically used for *reading* data from an app; a URL you visit in a regular fashion, by clicking a link for example, is a GET

---

[11] http://stackoverflow.com/questions/4410704/why-would-one-omit-the-close-tag

request. POST requests are usually used for saving some data to the server, such as creating new data in a database. For a refresher on requests and responses, see Chapter 1.

The `input` element is the button we'll click to save the comment — the `value` attribute is what is written on the button, while the `type` is there to make sure this button is used for submitting the form.

If you refresh http://guestbook.app now, you should see a Save button at the bottom of the screen. Clicking it will do nothing but refresh the screen (the button submits the form, but since there's no PHP logic to process the form, we're just redirected to the same page we were on).

Above the input, but still inside the form element, we add the following:

```
    <label>Name: <input type="text" name="name" placeholder="Your
➥ name"></label>
    <label>Email: <input type="text" name="email" placeholder="your@
➥email.com"></label>
    <label>Comment: <textarea name="comment" cols="30" rows="10">
➥</textarea></label>
```

HTML forms usually have labels for various form fields describing what's supposed to be entered into the field. A label often wraps an element—a tag goes on either side of it, like in the code above. The `type` attribute tells the browser it's a regular text field, the `name` is there so we can identify the value in the PHP code, and the `placeholder` is there to serve as an example of possible inputs. A `textarea` is a different kind of element with no `type`, just dimensions expressed in the form of columns (`cols`) and `rows`.

If we also remove the dummy outputs from the PHP part, we get a final result that looks like this:

```
<?php

require_once '../vendor/autoload.php';

$database = new medoo([
    'database_type' => 'sqlite',
    'database_file' => '../storage/database.db'
```

```
]);

?>

  ⋮

<form method="post">
    <label>Name: <input type="text" name="name" placeholder="Your
➥ name"></label>
    <label>Email: <input type="text" name="email" placeholder="your@
➥email.com"></label>
    <label>Comment: <textarea name="comment" cols="30" rows="10">
➥</textarea></label>
    <input type="submit" value="Save">
</form>
```

It looks like Figure 8.14 when seen in the browser.

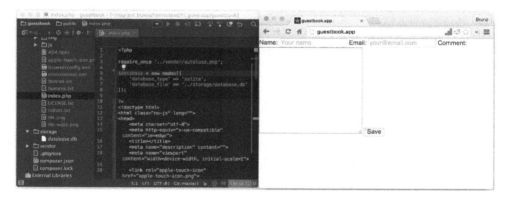

Figure 8.14. Form created

It's quite ugly, but we can deal with that later.

Second Push

With some additional files in the mix and our form built, it's time to do another Git push:

```
git add -A
git commit -m "Added HTML5 Boilerplate and built submission form"
git push origin master
```

Creating the Comment Class and the Database Table

Developing the Comment class from scratch with object oriented syntax, how ever
simple it may be, is outside the scope of this book. There are plenty of other books
you can look at for guidance on basic OOP — the links at the end of the chapter
will be helpful. Right now, just to get some PHP muscle memory, I would recommend
you type the code below into a new file called Comment.php which you should
create in the src subfolder of the root folder of our project (the src folder will need
to be created, too). Alternatively, if you really don't feel like it, the full code is copy-
pasteable at: http://bit.ly/sp-book-comment.

```php
<?php

namespace SitePoint;

class Comment
{
    protected $database;

    protected $name;
    protected $email;
    protected $comment;
    protected $submissionDate;

    public function __construct(\medoo $medoo)
    {
        $this->database = $medoo;
    }

    public function findAll()
    {
        $collection = [];
        $comments = $this->database->select('comments', '*',
            ["ORDER" => "comments.submissionDate DESC"]);
        if ($comments) {
            foreach ($comments as $array) {
                $comment = new self($this->database);
                $collection[] = $comment
```

```php
                    ->setComment($array['comment'])
                    ->setEmail($array['email'])
                    ->setName($array['name'])
                    ->setSubmissionDate($array['submissionDate']);
            }
        }

        return $collection;
    }

    public function setName($name)
    {
        $this->name = (string)$name;

        return $this;
    }

    public function setEmail($email)
    {
        if (filter_var($email, FILTER_VALIDATE_EMAIL)) {
            $this->email = $email;
        } else {
            throw new \InvalidArgumentException('Not a valid
➥ email!');
        }

        return $this;
    }

    public function setComment($comment)
    {
        if (strlen($comment) < 10) {
            throw new \InvalidArgumentException('Comment too
➥ short!');
        } else {
            $this->comment = $comment;
        }

        return $this;
    }

    protected function setSubmissionDate($date)
    {
        $this->submissionDate = $date;
```

```php
        return $this;
    }

    public function getName()
    {
        return $this->name;
    }

    public function getEmail()
    {
        return $this->email;
    }

    public function getComment()
    {
        return $this->comment;
    }

    public function getSubmissionDate()
    {
        return $this->submissionDate;
    }

    public function save()
    {
        if ($this->getName() && $this->getEmail() && $this->->getComment()) {
            $this->setSubmissionDate(date('Y-m-d H:i:s'));

            return $this->database->insert('comments', [
                'name' => $this->getName(),
                'email' => $this->getEmail(),
                'comment' => $this->getComment(),
                'submissionDate' => $this->getSubmissionDate()
            ]);
        }
        throw new \Exception("Failed to save!");
    }
}
```

 ## Explanation of the Code Above

An in-depth explanation of this class and all the functionality its code allows, along with upgrades to the app's functionality that go beyond what we're covering in the book, will be covered in bonus posts published on SitePoint.com. To find links to this bonus content, please see the repository with the source code of the guestbook app we're building at https://github.com/spbooks/phpenv1-example.

Before the Comment class can be used by our application, the app needs to know where the class is. Remember the namespaces section from Chapter 7? This is the part where we bind the namespace of the Comment class (namespace SitePoint;) to a physical location on the hard drive (the src folder). We must edit the **composer.json** file in our project's root folder and add the section:

```
"autoload": {
    "psr-4": {
        "SitePoint\\": "src"
    }
}
```

For reference, Figure 8.15 what the whole file now looks like:

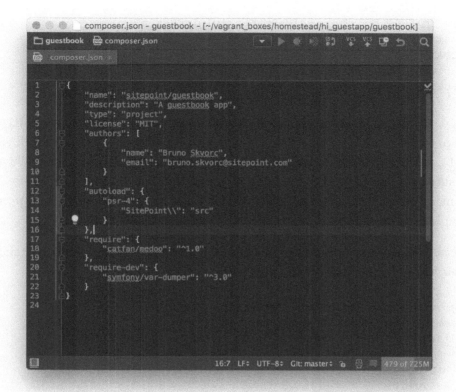

Figure 8.15. The current contents of **composer.json**

To apply these changes, we run `composer dump-autoload` so that the script which auto-includes classes is regenerated with the `src` folder in mind.

One last step: before we can save data into the database, we need to create a table into which the data will go. In the terminal, inside the root folder, execute:

```
sqlite3 storage/database.db
```

This enters the database in *CLI* mode, allowing for live execution of SQL commands. To create the table we want, we need to execute the following statement while inside the database engine:

```
CREATE TABLE comments (
  id INTEGER NOT NULL PRIMARY KEY AUTOINCREMENT,
  name TEXT NOT NULL,
  email TEXT NOT NULL,
  comment TEXT NOT NULL,
  submissionDate TEXT NOT NULL);
```

This will create a table called `comments` with an auto-incrementing integer ID (meaning the ID number will rise automatically as new records are inserted, we don't need to provide this value), a `name` field, an `email` field, a `comment` field, and our `submissionDate` field for saving the date of creation. Typing `.tables` after the command above is executed should show that the table was created. Exit the prompt by typing `.quit`.

How about we test everything we made so far? In **index.php**, under the `$database = new medoo...` block put the following:

```
$comment = new SitePoint\Comment($database);
$comment->setEmail('bruno@skvorc.me')
  ->setName('Bruno Skvorc')
  ->setComment('It works!')
  ->setComment('Hooray! Saving comments works!')
  ->save();
```

Refresh http://guestbook.app, and there shouldn't be any changes.

However, if we look inside our database, we should be able to see the saved comment, as shown in Figure 8.16.

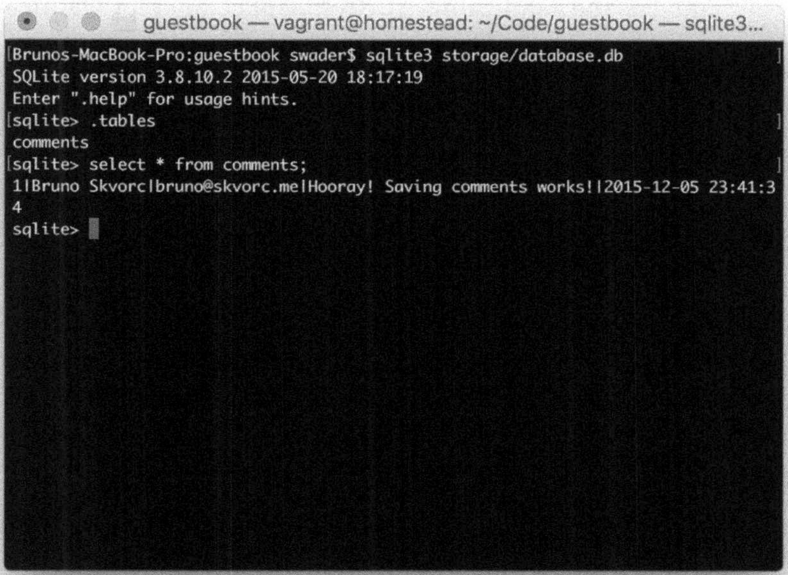

```
guestbook — vagrant@homestead: ~/Code/guestbook — sqlite3...
[Brunos-MacBook-Pro:guestbook swader$ sqlite3 storage/database.db
SQLite version 3.8.10.2 2015-05-20 18:17:19
Enter ".help" for usage hints.
[sqlite> .tables
comments
[sqlite> select * from comments;
1|Bruno Skvorc|bruno@skvorc.me|Hooray! Saving comments works!|2015-12-05 23:41:3
4
sqlite>
```

Figure 8.16. The comment is saved!

If by some chance the save didn't go through, this is where a call to the `var-dumper` might be helpful. After the call to `->save();`, in a new line, put:

```
dump($database->error());
```

If there were errors, this command will output them on the screen and you'll know exactly what went wrong.

Third Push

It's time to add, commit and push again. Try to recall the commands without looking them up. If you get stuck, they're a couple of pages back.

Development vs Production Database

It would be rather silly if we did all our testing on a real database, and then that ended up live for our users to see. We need a "development" database which will be in use while developing, and a "production" database which we'll deploy alongside our app. See the Application Environment chapter for clarifications on these terms.

There are many ways to do this, but one of the easiest is:

- app checks if a file called **database.local.db** exists
- if the file exists, it is used as the database
- if the file does not exist, the file **database.db** is used

The file `database.local.db` can be put into the `.gitignore` file so it never ends up being shared with other team members, and so that it cannot end up in the repo (thus never getting deployed via Git). By default, this will make the production version of our app use the production database, and the local version of our app use the development database.

First, let's empty the database of dummy data.

```
sqlite3 storage/database.db
delete from comments;
delete from sqlite_sequence where name='comments';
```

The first `delete` deletes all test rows we may have inserted. The second one resets the auto-incrementing ID field back to 0. Now, let's turn this database file into a template for future ones, then create the databases we need:

```
cd storage
cp database.db database.tpl.db
cp database.tpl.db database.local.db
cd ..
```

cp is a terminal command for "Copy".

There should now be three files: `database.tpl.db`, `database.db` and `database.local.db`.

We can now add **database.local.db** to our **.gitignore** file, which will make sure it never ends up in the repository:

```
echo -e "\ndatabase.local.db" >> .gitignore
```

Finally, let's edit **index.php**. We'll replace the Medoo initialization:

```
$database = new medoo([
    'database_type' => 'sqlite',
    'database_file' => '../storage/database.db'
]);
```

with:

```
$file = '../storage/database.db';
if (is_writable('../storage/database.local.db')) {
    $file = '../storage/database.local.db';
}
$database = new medoo([
    'database_type' => 'sqlite',
    'database_file' => $file
]);
```

The above translates into "If there is a writable file called **database.local.db** in the folder one level above the current one, use that. Otherwise, use `database.db`".

If we now refresh `http://guestbook.app` (and the dummy comment creation code is still there), we should see the comment appear in **database.local.db**, but not in **database.db**, as shown in Figure 8.17.

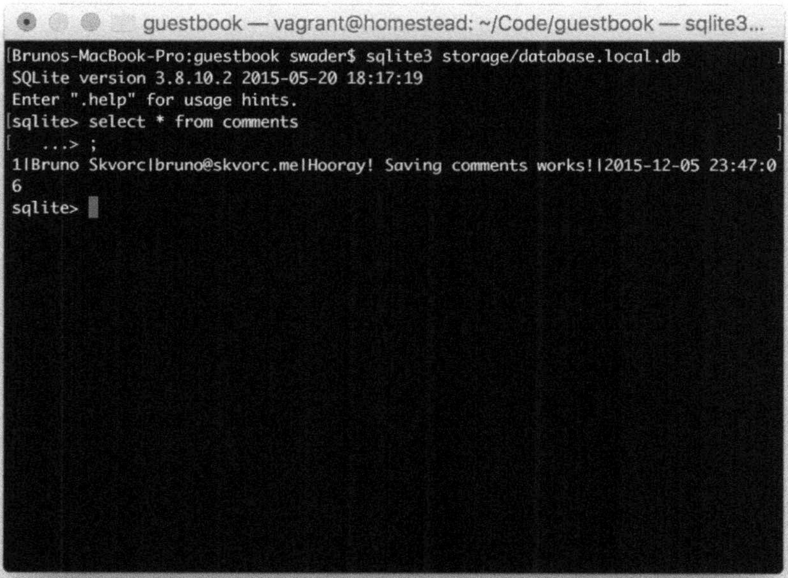

Figure 8.17. Local database populated

Fourth Push

Again, add, commit, and push. Don't look up the commands. If you can't remember them, rather than look them up on the previous pages, try Googling for them. Finding solutions by simply searching for them will become a daily ordeal for you in the very near future. True skill is not in knowing something, but in knowing where to find that knowledge (though, in all honesty, you'll probably end up on StackOverflow).

Posting and Displaying Comments

First, let's modify **index.php** by removing the dummy Comment creation logic. The PHP section and, thus, our new starting point, looks like this now:

```
<?php

require_once '../vendor/autoload.php';
```

```php
$file = '../storage/database.db';
if (is_writable('../storage/database.local.db')) {
    $file = '../storage/database.local.db';
}
$database = new medoo([
    'database_type' => 'sqlite',
    'database_file' => $file
]);
$comment = new SitePoint\Comment($database);

?>
```

At this point, we have autoloading set up, we have a database instance configured, and we have an instance of the Comment class with the database connection injected into it..

First up, let's make it possible to post new comments.

Posting

As we said earlier, when we visit a URL in a browser, we issue a GET request. GET requests are for reading, they're not supposed to alter data. This is why our submission form is using method="post", so that the request we send to our app after submitting the form is a POST one. In PHP, there are constructs called **superglobals** — variables (usually arrays) accessible at any level of the application. Two such superglobals are $_GET and $_POST.

When we visit a URL like http://some.url.com/?var=something&name=something-else, the $_GET superglobal array will look like this:

```php
$_GET = [
    'var' => 'something',
    'name' => 'something-else'
];
```

In other words, we'll be able to access var and name from the URL in any part of the application with an approach like $username = $_GET['name'].

$_POST does the same thing, but for values submitted via a POST request, such as from a form. When a form has an input field with the name name, then the $_POST superglobal will also have a `name` key which will contain the value of said field. Thus, the fields we defined in our form will have their values represented in `$_POST` after the form has been submitted, as we'll soon see.

First, we need to detect we're dealing with a form submission. Under the `$comment` line, but before the closing `?>` PHP tag, we put the following:

```php
if ($_SERVER['REQUEST_METHOD'] === 'POST') {
    echo "Form was submitted!";
}
```

The first line detects that we're dealing with a form submission. Remember how we used `method='post'` in our HTML on the `<form>` element? `$_SERVER` is another superglobal in PHP containing information about the current request that's coming in (it gets filled automatically). In this case, we're dealing with the request that was submitted via a form, thus using the POST method.

If we refresh http://guestbook.app now, we should see nothing new. But if we press the **Save** button on the form, we should see "Form was submitted!". There's a small problem, though. If we try to refresh the page after a form submission, we'll get a strange warning, shown in Figure 8.18.

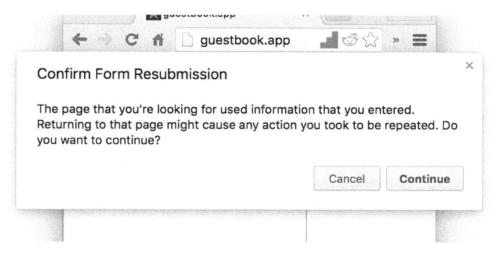

Figure 8.18. Form resubmission

In Chrome's universe, a refresh means a complete redo—the repeat of the last step, rather than re-rendering the URL we're on. It wants to re-send the form information in its entirety when we try to refresh. This doesn't happen if we punch in the http://guestbook.app URL manually and re-visit it that way, but refreshing it after a form submission will always produce this warning. You'll encounter this on other websites, too. We don't want to scare our visitors with this message, so we'll work around it. For now, let's process the submission.

Replace `echo "Form was submitted!";` with:

```
dump($_POST);
```

Then, enter some data into the comment form and submit it. You should see something similar to Figure 8.19.

Figure 8.19. Dump of post data

Notice how all three fields were dumped (the `dump` function is the functionality of the symfony/var-dumper package we installed at the beginning of this chapter), and have the same names as the fields from which they originate.

An important aspect of receiving data from untrusted users in systems like the ones we're building is *input validation*.

Validation: Never Trust User Input!

The golden rule of validation is *never trust user input*, because you never know when someone well versed in coding will stumble upon your app and attempt to enter malicious information into the fields in an attempt to break your app (by, for example, entering data which triggers commands in the database, also known as SQL injection[12]).

There are many ways to validate input data, and in this case we'll be using a minimalist package called `particle/validator`. Let's install it.

```
composer require particle/validator
```

Above the `require_once` line, put:

```
use Particle\Validator\Validator;
```

This imports the class so we can use its shorter name. Then, replace `dump($_POST)` with:

```
$v = new Validator();
$v->required('name')->lengthBetween(1, 100)->alnum(true);
$v->required('email')->email()->lengthBetween(5, 255);
$v->required('comment')->lengthBetween(10, null);

$result = $v->validate($_POST);

if ($result->isValid()) {
    echo "Submission is good!";
} else {
    dump($result->getMessages());
}
```

The Validator package in question uses rules to define some constraints on certain values in an array. In this case, we made all three fields required with `required()`, we set a limit on their length with `lengthBetween`, we forced the name to be alphanumeric (so no miscellaneous characters, like punctuation — but spaces are allowed, indicated by the `true` we passed in) and we forced the email to be verified as an email format. Just for testing, we dump the errors we get if something goes wrong, or output "Submission is good" if all fields are OK. Figure 8.20 shows what I get when I enter an invalid email address:

---

[12] https://www.owasp.org/index.php/SQL_Injection

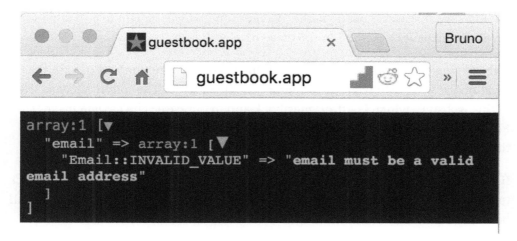

Figure 8.20. Invalid email address

With our input data validated, we're ready to save the comment into the database. Replace echo "Submission is good!"; with:

```
try {
    $comment
        ->setName($_POST['name'])
        ->setEmail($_POST['email'])
        ->setComment($_POST['comment'])
        ->save();

    header('Location: /');
    return;

    } catch (\Exception $e) {
        die($e->getMessage());
}
```

The try/catch block is another advanced construct. Suffice it to say that *anything thrown can be caught*. In the Comment class, we tend to throw new exceptions of different types. When an exception is thrown (**throwing an exception** in PHP basically means "making PHP crash with a specific error message), it bubbles up, which means that the whole application can detect it, all the way up to the root **index.php** file. This is why, in **index.php**, we put the try safeguard around all the $comment method calls; if one of them throws an exception, the catch block will trigger. The logic in the catch block will simply kill PHP with the function die() and output the message that was passed via the \Exception that was caught (e.g. "Failed to save!" in the save() method in the Comment class).

If the saving executes flawlessly, we call the header() function and pass in the location for where we want the browser to redirect us to. The "path" / means "root of this website", which is http://guestbook.app in our case. The return makes sure PHP's code execution stops there. Why did we do this? Because of the aforementioned "form resubmission on refresh" problem.[13]

If we now enter valid information into the form and press submit, we'll be sent back to http://guestbook.app, the comment will appear in the database, and the page will be refreshable without the warning.

Try it out. Enter a couple of comments and take a look inside the database with:

```
sqlite3 database.local.db
select * from comments;
```

Reading

All we need to do now is add the listing logic to our app; we want to list the currently saved comments.

Above the entire form block in **index.php**, put the following:

```php
<?php foreach ($comment->findAll() as $comment) : ?>

    <div class="comment">
        <h3>On <?= $comment->getSubmissionDate() ?>, <?= $comment->
➥getName() ?> wrote:</h3>

        <p><?= $comment->getComment(); ?></p>
    </div>

<?php endforeach; ?>
```

When mixing PHP and HTML, we can use colon (:) and the appropriate *block closer* instead of using curly braces { }. This helps maintain sanity when dealing with

---

[13] The **header** function can only work if it comes **before** any HTML output. Thus, we've put all our PHP code at the top of the file.

big files — one doesn't have to strain one's eyes looking for closing braces. Every `for` has its `endfor`, `if` has its `endif`, `foreach` has an `endforeach`, and so on. It's a convenience, a bit of syntactic sugar.

In the code above, we call the `findAll` method on `$comment`, the method which fetches all the comments from the database in reverse order of submission (newest to oldest). Then, we create an HTML div block to contain our comment. Inside it we have an `h3` element for the comment's "title" (information on who wrote the comment and when) followed by a `p` element, which will contain our comment's text.

The structure `<?= $variable ?>` is short for `<?php echo $variable ?>`, and is available in all modern PHP version at all times (note that this is **not** the same as short open tags[14]).

That's it — it was *that* simple. Let's test our code by refreshing http://guestbook.app, as shown in Figure 8.21.

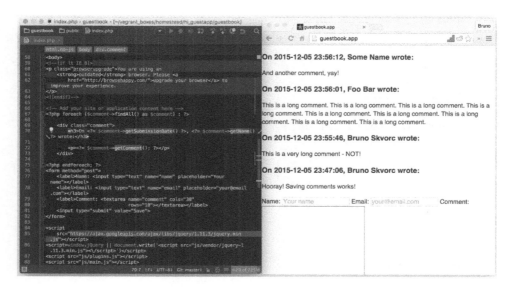

Figure 8.21. It works!

---

[14] http://php.net/manual/en/ini.core.php#ini.short-open-tag

CSS

Throughout all this the only thing we haven't paid any attention to was the design. Let's drop in some rudimentary CSS, just to make everything prettier. Under the line `<link rel="stylesheet" href="css/main.css">`, add this one:

```
<link rel="stylesheet" href="css/custom.css">
```

Then, create the file **public/css/custom.css** and give it the following contents (or paste from http://bit.ly/envbook-style):

```css
body {
    padding: 10px;
}

form {
    width: 500px;
    border: 1px solid silver;
    border-radius: 3px;
    padding: 10px 10px 10px 4px;
}

form > input {
    width: 100%;
    margin-left:4px;
    height: 35px;
    border: 1px solid silver;
    background: #cccccc;
}

form > input:hover {
    background: whitesmoke;
}

label {
    display: block;
    margin: 5px;
    color: grey;
}

label > input {
    line-height: 30px;
}
```

```
label > * {
    display: block;
    width: 100%;
}

.comment {
    width: 500px;
    border: 1px solid silver;
    border-radius: 3px;
    margin: 10px 0;
    background-color: lemonchiffon;
}

.comment > h3 {
    margin: 0;
    border-bottom: 1px solid silver;
    background-color: lightblue;
    padding: 3px;
}

.comment > p {
    margin: 10px;
}
```

This turns our ugly app into something marginally easier to look at, as shown in Figure 8.22.

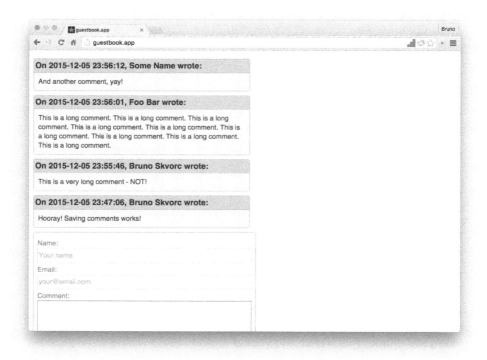

Figure 8.22. A prettier app

Final Push

By now, you should be a master of the push flow. Do one final push, and our application is in the repository in its final form.

Deployment

In this section, we'll deploy our most excellent app. For more theory behind deployment, see Chapter 6.

Deploying on a Shared Host (Hostgator)

Like we discussed in Chapter 6, shared hosting isn't really a good option. It's insecure, often very limited in resources (despite the *unlimited* claims) and these days not all that cheaper than VPS. Still, it might be the only thing you have access to, so it only makes sense we cover an old school FTP deployment procedure.

Shared hosts will often have cPanel as a means of managing one's server, not unlike the one shown in Figure 8.23.

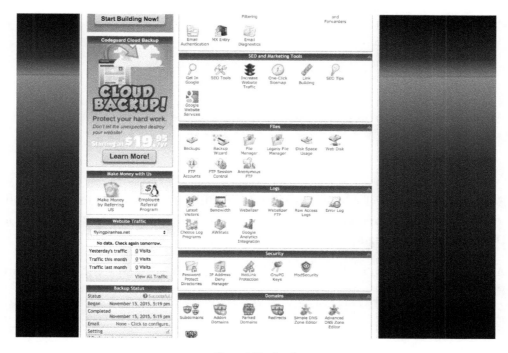

Figure 8.23. cPanel

In this case, we're using Hostgator[15], but the procedure is almost identical on every shared host.

To deploy an app, you'll need a domain. Domains can be purchased (or rather, rented) on websites like http://namecheap.com or http://name.com, and can range from $2 per year to $2000 per year and more. I'll pick one of my own domains that I'm not using for this example: caimeo.com. Add your domain to your shared host via the **Addon domains** dialog:

[15] http://hostgator.com

Create an Addon Domain

New Domain Name: caimeo.com

Subdomain or FTP Username: caimeo

Document Root: /caimeo.com

Password: ••••••••••••••••••••

Password (Again): ••••••••••••••••••••

Strength (Why?): Very Strong (100/100)   Password Generator

Add Domain

IMPORTANT: Your web host must enable this feature for your account before you can use it. Addon domains will not function unless you register your domain and configure it to point to the correct DNS servers.

Figure 8.24. Adding a new domain

Each shared host will also instruct you how to configure DNS settings for the domain to respond to the shared host's servers. Note that it might take up to 24 hours for a DNS change to **propagate** (apply) across the web.

Adding a new domain will automatically create an FTP account for it, as shown in Figure 8.25.

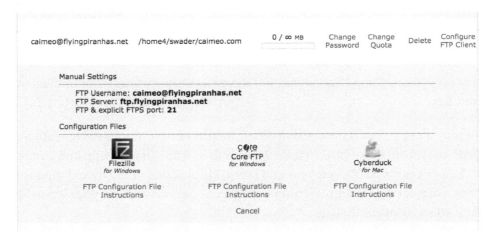

caimeo@flyingpiranhas.net   /home4/swader/caimeo.com   0 / ∞ MB   Change Password   Change Quota   Delete   Configure FTP Client

Manual Settings

FTP Username: **caimeo@flyingpiranhas.net**
FTP Server: **ftp.flyingpiranhas.net**
FTP & explicit FTPS port: **21**

Configuration Files

Filezilla
for Windows

Core FTP
for Windows

Cyberduck
for Mac

FTP Configuration File Instructions

FTP Configuration File Instructions

FTP Configuration File Instructions

Cancel

Figure 8.25. New FTP account created

Note that the core domain behind the FTP account is different purely because my Hostgator account was originally opened on it. There are ways to change a primary domain, but the process is too time consuming and intense to be worth the effort.

The next step is downloading an FTP client; this example will use Filezilla[16], but you can use whichever clientyou prefer. In the **Site Manager** window, we add a new site and enter the credentials given to us by Hostgator, as shown in Figure 8.26.

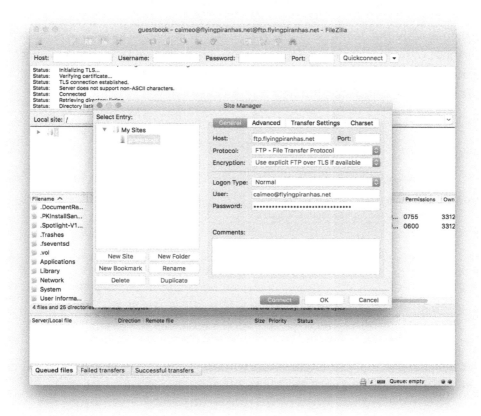

Figure 8.26. Configured in Filezilla

You might be asked to "trust a certificate" when connecting. If so, just confirm.

Once the connection goes through, the right side indicating **Remote** will show an empty folder — in reality, the location is a subfolder of your home folder on the shared host's server. To begin, we'll first upload our app by finding it in the left frame, and dragging it over into the right one.

---

[16] https://filezilla-project.org/

Due to having to copy the entire vendor folder and everything we used in development, this might take a while — there's no proper way to cherry pick what gets copied, really. When this is done, we'll need to delete some of the development files and folders (**.git,**, **.gitignore**, **database.local.db**, etc.) manually.

We then modify the document root of the domain to lead to `caimeo.com/guest-book/public` rather than the default `caimeo.com`, as shown in Figure 8.27, because otherwise our app won't run at http://caimeo.com, but rather at http://caimeo.com/guestbook/public.

Figure 8.27. Modify docroot

After the changes apply (it might take a while), we should be able to visit our app at the main domain, and we'll be able to enter new comments, too!

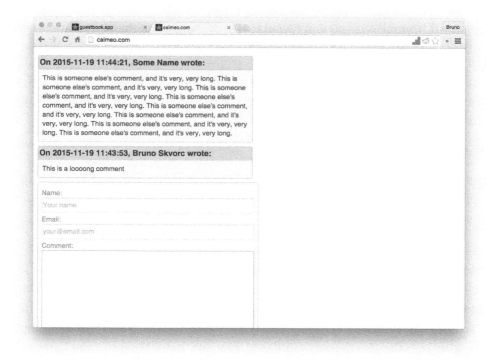

Figure 8.28. Caimeo.com with comments

Victory!

The app is now deployed live on a shared host and works like a charm. It's a bit tedious to have to reupload all changed files manually, and the app isn't all that secure, but it's good enough for demos and proof-of-concept apps.

Deploying on DigitalOcean

Time for the good stuff.

On DigitalOcean, a VPS provider, you're given the ability to create **droplets**. A droplet is a virtual private server that's very easy to tear down and rebuild, much like a Vagrant box, only performing much better. DigitalOcean bills you according to the resources a droplet spends, so unless you intend to host a long running application, it makes sense to tear it down after you're done with it to conserve credits.

An added benefit of this type of setup is that you don't have to get a domain just to launch a site — DigitalOcean supports (as do most VPS hosts, as a matter of fact)

IP-based access, so you can access your app by punching in an IP bound to your droplet. Additionally, if you don't want to use DigitalOcean, the procedure is nearly identical on every VPS; in all cases, you're dealing with a typical blank server!

Droplets can be as cheap as $5 per month and by using someone's referral link, you can get $10 instantly. Here's my link if you'd like to give the deployment procedure below a try: http://bit.ly/doref.[17]

New Droplet

Assuming you've set up a new account and have some credits, let's create a new droplet by going to https://cloud.digitalocean.com/droplets/new, giving it a name, and selecting:

- $5 per month
- the region nearest to you
- Ubuntu 14.04 image (it's the same OS that Homestead Improved uses, helping development-production parity and providing us with a familiar environment)
- No SSH key. We'll receive a root password via email which we'll use for remotely logging into the server (very similar to `vagrant ssh`). We'll use the latter approach, considering most readers will likely be without SSH keys. For additional information on setting up SSH keys and proper security measures, Digital Ocean's tutorial[18] will be invaluable.

Once the droplet has been created, you should have access to its main dashboard, shown in Figure 8.29.

---

[17] Full disclosure: the owner of the referral link (that's me!) will receive $25 as soon as a person they referred spends $25 of their own, not counting the initial free $10.

[18] https://www.digitalocean.com/community/tutorials/how-to-configure-ssh-key-based-authentication-on-a-freebsd-server

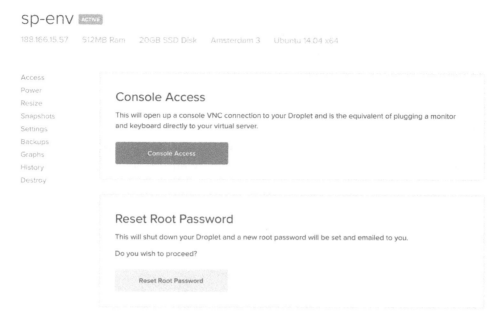

sp-env [ACTIVE]

188.166.15.57   512MB Ram   20GB SSD Disk   Amsterdam 3   Ubuntu 14.04 x64

Access
Power
Resize
Snapshots
Settings
Backups
Graphs
History
Destroy

Console Access

This will open up a console VNC connection to your Droplet and is the equivalent of plugging a monitor and keyboard directly to your virtual server.

[Console Access]

Reset Root Password

This will shut down your Droplet and a new root password will be set and emailed to you.

Do you wish to proceed?

[Reset Root Password]

Figure 8.29. Droplet dashboard

Notice the IP address right underneath its name. Right now, it won't lead anywhere if it's put in your browser's URL field. We can, however, use it to log into our server (whenever you see IP-ADDRESS below, substitute for the IP of your own droplet):

```
ssh root@IP-ADDRESS
```

Use the password from the email when prompted. As soon as you're logged in, you will be asked to change the root password. Change it to something familiar but not easily guessable. My recommendation would be using a password manager to generate a random one, and then just paste from there in the future.

Once you're in the server, a welcome message might display a warning about locales. This can be fixed by running:

```
sudo locale-gen en_US en_US.UTF-8
export LANG=en_US.UTF-8
export LC_ALL=en_US.UTF-8
```

What this does is tell the OS on the droplet (Ubuntu Linux) which language we're using (US English), and the type of encoding used to display its characters. UTF-8 is a type of encoding which makes possible the use of letters of different alphabets and similar miscellaneous characters. UTF-8 is outside the scope of this book and chapter, but if you're curious, there's an absolutely essential (and newbie-friendly) bit of writing from 2003 about it at the following link: http://www.joelonsoftware.com/articles/Unicode.html

If your local computer is running OS X or Linux, there might be another setting you might need to modify. Exit the droplet with `exit`, then edit the file `ssh_config` in `/etc/ssh/`, and comment out the following line by putting a hash in front:

```
# SendEnv LANG LC_*
```

This is due to a common remote access bug[19].

Now we're ready to install prerequisite software.

Prerequisites

First, we need to have Ubuntu pull in a list of the newly available Ubuntu packages. While you're logged into the droplet, run:

```
sudo apt-get update
```

With the list updated, let's start by installing Git, SQLite3, and Nginx:

```
sudo apt-get install git sqlite3 nginx
```

Suddenly, our IP address is live! (Figure 8.30).

---

[19] http://askubuntu.com/a/530829

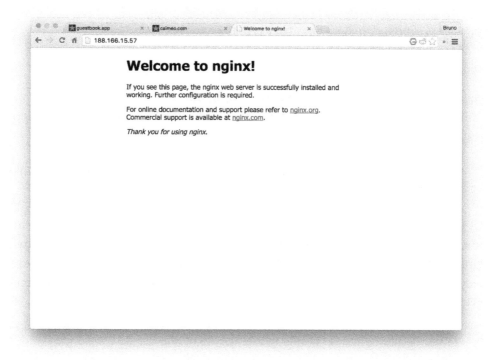

Figure 8.30. Nginx welcome page

Next, we need to install PHP.

PHP and Composer

To install PHP, we run:

```
sudo add-apt-repository ppa:ondrej/php5-5.6
sudo apt-get update
sudo apt-get install php5 php5-fpm php5-cli php5-sqlite
```

php5 is the core PHP program. php5-fpm is the web interface through which a server like Nginx passes PHP files and gets back a response. php5-cli is the command line interface, so we can use PHP in the terminal, without the browser. This is what Composer uses to work. php5-sqlite is, of course, a PHP extension for communication with SQLite3, which we know we'll be needing.

To install Composer globally, like on Homestead Improved, we execute:

```
curl -sS https://getcomposer.org/installer | php
sudo mv composer.phar /usr/local/bin/composer
```

Server Configuration

To configure Nginx, we can just grab the configuration from our VM! Open a new terminal tab or window on the host machine, enter the Vagrant VM we developed the app on with **vagrant ssh** as usual, and execute:

```
cp /etc/nginx/sites-available/guestbook.app ~/Code/guestbook-nginx.
➥txt
```

This will make the server configuration file immediately available in the VM's main folder. Open it, select its contents (but be careful to ignore or just delete the two bottom lines — those mentioning SSL), copy the selection to the clipboard, and then *while connected to the droplet* (switch back to the window / terminal connected to it) run:

```
vim /etc/nginx/sites-available/guestbook.app
```

Press the **i** key to enter *insert* mode, and paste the contents in there with **Ctrl + V** (**CMD + V** on a Mac). Then, edit the following lines:

- change the value of **server_name** from a name (**guestbook.app**) to the IP of the droplet
- change the value of **root** to **/var/www/guestbook/public**

The **var/www/** folder is the location that's typically used to host applications on Linux. Exit *insert* mode with Esc, then exit the file by typing **:x** and pressing Enter.

Then, reboot Nginx with:

```
sudo service nginx restart
```

 ### Encountering Issues

If you run into problems like a fully white screen, or a cryptic error, check the error logs by running **tail -f /var/log/nginx/guestbook.app-error.log**. Tail outputs the "tail" of a file (its last 10 lines) and **-f** tells it to "watch this file and update output as it changes", meaning that as new errors come in, they'll immediately show up on screen. Feel free to open another terminal window, connect to the droplet through it just like above, and run the `tail` there; that way, you still have full control over the main terminal window to run commands in, and the second will monitor errors for you.

Pulling With Git

At last! We're ready to deploy our app!

```
cd /var/www
git clone https://github.com/spbooks/phpenv1-example guestbook
cd guestbook
composer install --no-dev -o
```

Notice how we used `--no-dev` to prevent installing the `dev` packages and make the installation faster. On an application of this size, it hardly matters, but on bigger projects, the difference is obvious. We also used the option `-o` which is short for `--optimize-autoloader` and builds a *classmap* - a special file which turns all namespace-to-classes combinations (from the `autoload` section of `composer.json`) into a fixed pre-calculated array, which in most cases significantly speeds up autoloading. Read more about these command line options in the docs[20].

Seeing as we did all this with the `root` account (we logged in with `root@IP-ADDRESS`, remember?), our application is "owned" by the root user because that user created it. This is okay in most cases, but not when PHP needs to do some reading and writing on the hard drive; PHP is running as a separate user, and a user cannot modify a super-user's (root's) files. As a final step, we need to modify permissions:

```
d /var/www/guestbook
sudo chown -R :www-data .
sudo chmod -R 775 storage
```

The `chown` command gives ownership of the folder to the `www-data` group of users: a special subset of user accounts on the server in charge of serving web pages (PHP and Nginx belong to this group). The `chmod` option gives writing permissions on

---

[20] https://getcomposer.org/doc/03-cli.md

the entire `storage` folder to its owner (root) and owning group (`www-data`). In both cases `-R` means "recursive", which means "apply to all subfolders as well".[21]

If we test our app now, we should see that everything is working fine, as shown in Figure 8.31.

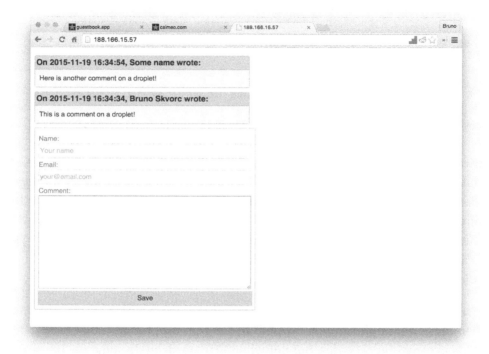

Figure 8.31. A working droplet

Conclusion

This chapter put to practice all the theory we covered before. Pretty much every term we discussed and every code snippet we tried out were used in one way or another through the creation of our little app.

---

[21] 775 is a file/folder access code—read more about them in this LinuxQuestions forum post: http://www.linuxquestions.org/questions/linux-software-2/chmod-codes-list-142654/.

The final application (downloadable / cloneable here[22]), while nothing to admire, is a fine introduction to the modern development workflow. Of course, this is the mere bottom of the basics, and your mission, should you choose to accept it, will be to consume countless courses and tutorials more before even beginning to feel ready. Thanks to this book, however, you should have a solid foundation on which to build.

I encourage you to go through this chapter a couple more times. Start from scratch, follow the procedure, try to skip reading a step now and then and recall how it was done. Try to understand what the code does, really read into it. Once you've got it down and the guestbook is almost muscle memory, try and introduce a change. Look into styling your form with CSS, check out the links below to find out about OOP, unit testing, login systems. Build on this sample app and use it as your Frankenstein's monster, glue on new features, staple an arm or two onto its forehead. Most importantly: have fun! The more fun you have, the more you'll want to learn, experiment, and explore, and that's all becoming a programmer really is. Additionally, for bonus content, code explanations and tutorials on how to implement some other, more advanced features, please see the README file of the aforementioned repository.

For Those Who Want More

To learn about HTML and CSS:

- https://developer.mozilla.org/en-US/docs/Web/Guide/HTML/Introduction
- https://www.sitepoint.com/premium/courses/introduction-to-html-2897
- http://www.csstutorial.net/css-intro/introductioncss-part1.php
- http://www.sitepoint.com/web-foundations/introduction-css-selectors/
- https://www.sitepoint.com/premium/books/jump-start-css/online/ch01

To learn about modern PHP and MySQL:

- https://www.codecademy.com/learn/php
- http://knpuniversity.com/tracks/php
- https://laracasts.com/series/object-oriented-bootcamp-in-php
- https://laracasts.com/series/solid-principles-in-php

---

[22] https://github.com/spbooks/phpenv1-example

To learn about the basics of automatic testing:

- https://leanpub.com/mlaphp
- http://www.sitepoint.com/tag/phpunit
- https://knpuniversity.com/screencast/behat
- http://www.sitepoint.com/php-continuous-integration-travis-ci/

To learn about the Laravel framework, it's best if you look at https://laracasts.com/, while for Symfony, you'd best check out what http://knpuniversity.com has to offer.

Finally, to automate the last step of this chapter — deployment — and set it up so it happens every time you, for example, push to the master branch (and for the various names these procedures share), see:

- http://stackoverflow.com/questions/28608015/
- http://www.sitepoint.com/whats-continuous-deployment/
- http://www.sitepoint.com/php-continuous-integration-travis-ci/
- http://www.sitepoint.com/deploying-php-apps-digitalocean-dploy-io/
- http://www.sitepoint.com/deploy-symfony-apps-capifony/
- http://www.sitepoint.com/one-click-app-deployment-server-side-git-hooks/

For a constantly updated version of this list, see the README file of the example's repository at https://github.com/spbooks/phpenv1-example, or read http://phptherightway.com.

Lightning Source UK Ltd.
Milton Keynes UK
UKHW031822140422
401576UK00004B/205